AF574271

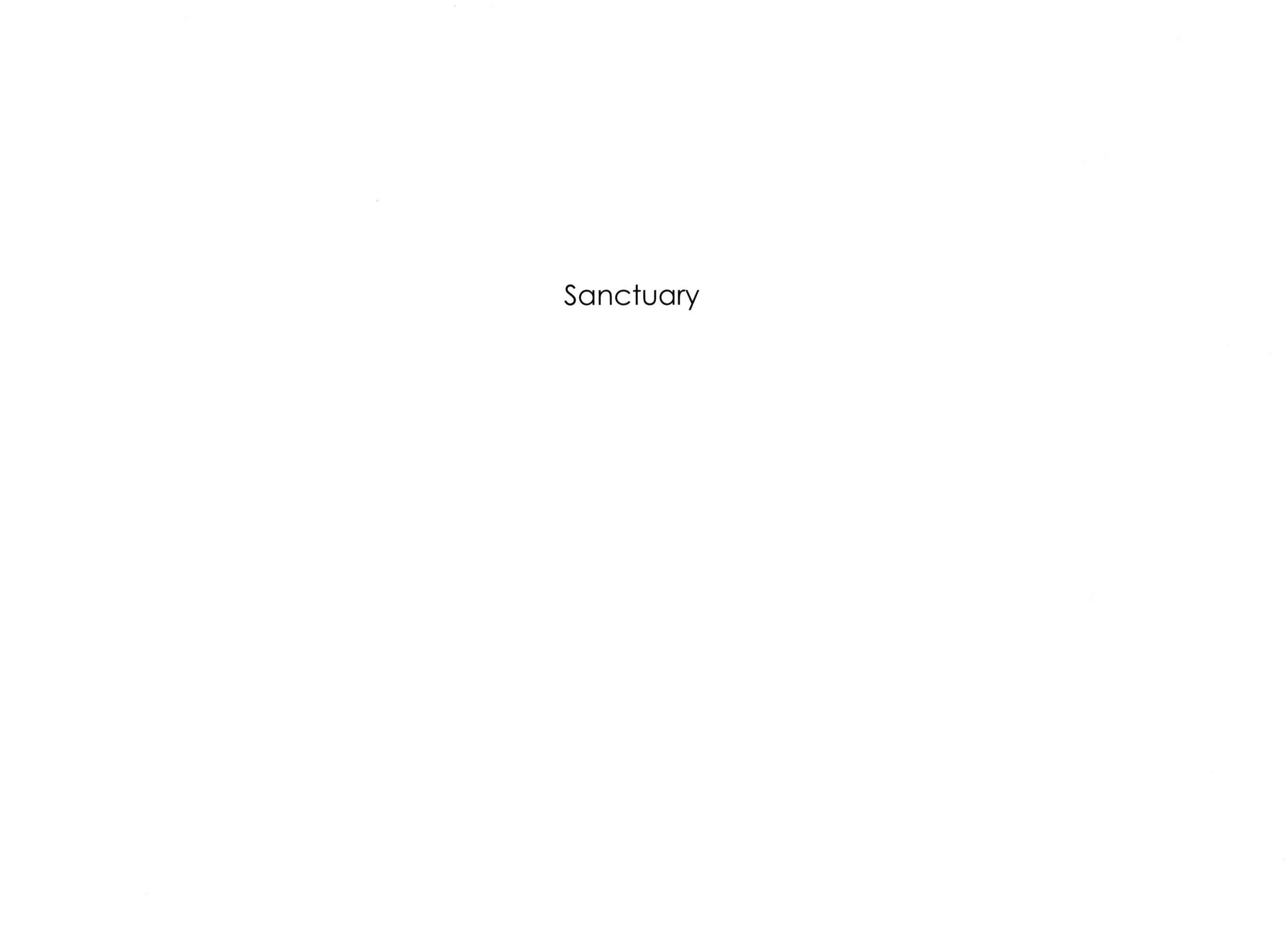

Sanctuary

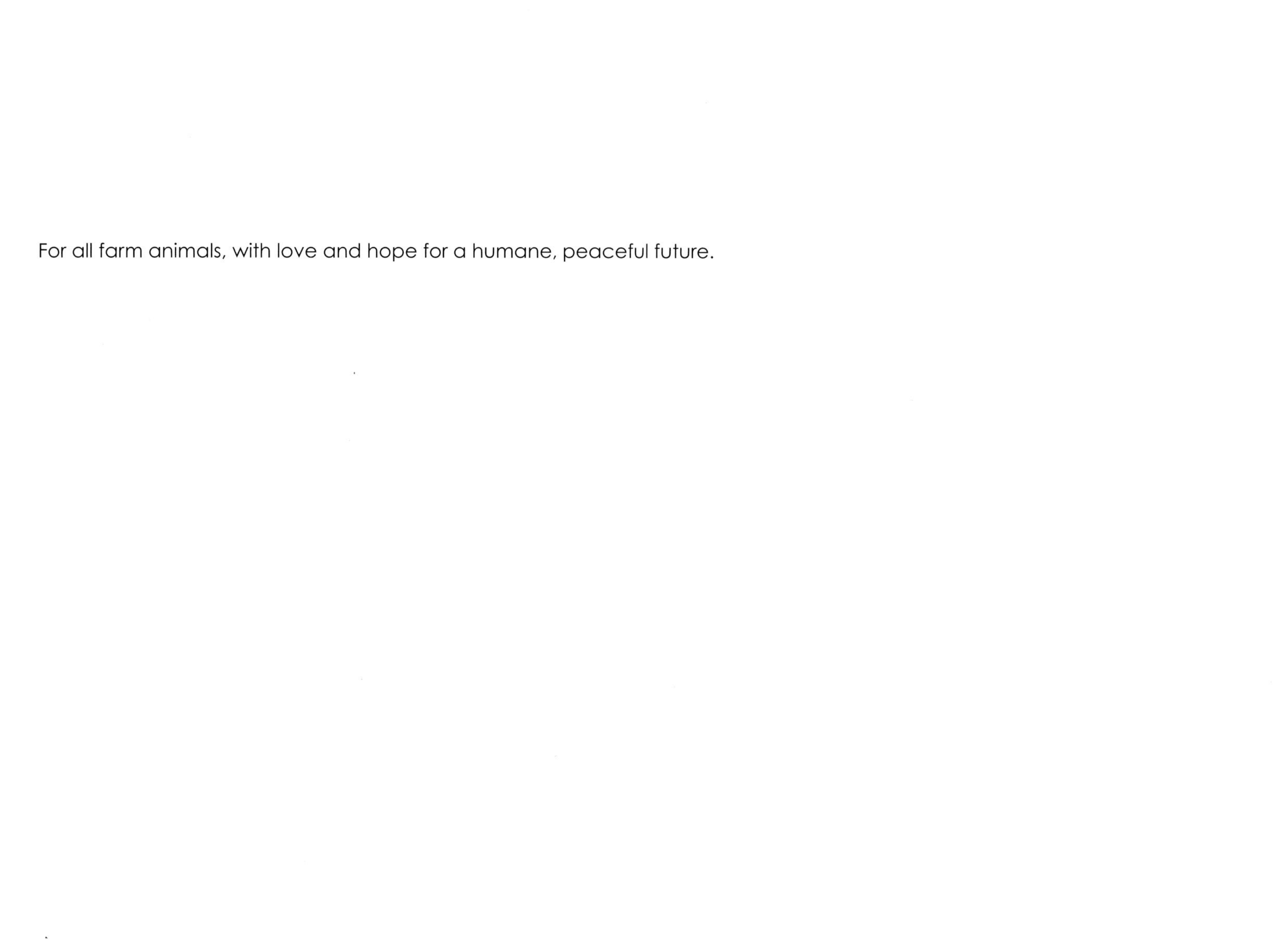

For all farm animals, with love and hope for a humane, peaceful future.

Sharon Lee Hart

Sanctuary

Portraits of Rescued Farm Animals

CHARTA

Design
Fayçal Zaouali

Editorial Coordination
Filomena Moscatelli

Copyediting
Luisa Nitrato Izzo

Copywriting and Press Office
Silvia Palombi

International Editorial Director
Francesca Sorace

Promotion and Web
Elisa Legnai

Distribution
Anna Visaggi

Administration
Grazia De Giosa

Warehouse and Outlet
Roberto Curiale

© 2012
Edizioni Charta, Milano
© Sharon Lee Hart for her works
© The authors for their texts

All rights reserved
ISBN 978-88-8158-845-9
Printed in Italy

Cover
Aintcho, Resident of Kindred Spirits Sanctuary, 2009

Back Cover
Unnamed Rooster (just arrived), Grateful Acres Sanctuary, 2009

No part of this publication may be reproduced, stored in a retrieval system or transmitted in any form or by any means without the prior permission in writing of copyright holders and of the publisher.

Edizioni Charta srl
Milano
via della Moscova, 27 - 20121
Tel. +39-026598098/026598200
Fax +39-026598577
e-mail: charta@chartaartbooks.it
www.chartaartbooks.it

Acknowledgements
Many thanks to those who helped make this book possible:
My family, especially my dad, Bill Hart, for his love and support; Gene Baur, Kathy Stevens, Karen Davis and Jeff Masson; all of the dedicated folks who work tirelessly on behalf of animals at Farm Sanctuary, Star Gazing Farm, United Poultry Concerns, Kindred Spirits Sanctuary, Poplar Spring Animal Sanctuary, Woodstock Sanctuary, Catskill Animal Sanctuary, Safe Haven Farm Sanctuary, SASHA Farm, and Grateful Acres; and the University of Kentucky for the support grant that enabled me to complete this project.

All photographs in this book were made over a two-year time period in 2009-10.

Contents

Foreword

Sharon Lee Hart's photography project *SANCTUARY* will take you on a journey to meet wonderful animals and the courageous rescuers who become their companions. Sanctuaries do more for advancing the cause of animals than anything else. First they save the lives of the individual animals; then they allow others to see for themselves how each and every animal at a shelter is a unique individual with a history as valuable (to the individual) as our own histories. Rich and famous human animals get to write their autobiographies, or have them written for them. But we all acknowledge that in fact, every human on earth deserves his or her own biography. The same is true for animals. As Tom Regan so memorably put it: "They too [animals] must be viewed as the experiencing subjects of a life, with inherent value of their own." (*The Case for Animal Rights*, University of California Press, Berkeley: 1985.) Each and every animal is as worthy of a biography as any human. And when you consider that the animals rarely do harm to other beings, they are probably more deserving. What most people discover when they visit a sanctuary is that all these animals share most, if not all, human emotions. As I have sat next to these residents, something else occurred to me that is somewhat heretical, not to say outrageous, at least to some. This: That in certain respects, some animals may be our emotional superiors. Dogs are more friendly; cats more contented; birds more gregarious; swans more faithful; elephants grieve more deeply, and so on. You can add to the list. I love it that there are more sanctuaries every year, all over the world, and that more people are visiting them. Some come away with a promise: "I will no longer participate in the suffering of these innocent creatures. From now on, I will eat no animal or, even better, no animal product."

This book by Sharon Lee Hart brings you directly into the lives of the animals she has photographed. You know that she has done so with respect and with love. This is not "voyeurism" but a chance to come directly into contact with animals that are living, breathing beings, as Sharon has experienced them. I hope that by seeing what Sharon has been able to achieve with her camera (and her heart), you will be inspired to visit one of the sanctuaries featured in the volume and see for yourself the animals whose expressive, poignant photographic portraits are included here.

Jeffrey Moussaieff Masson

Jeffrey Masson has a PhD from Harvard University. From 1970-79 he was professor of Sanskrit at the University of Toronto. He trained as a Freudian analyst and was briefly director of the Freud Archives in 1980-81. He is the author of 26 books, many of them focused on the emotional lives of animals. He currently lives in Auckland, New Zealand, with his wife, Leila (a pediatrician), two boys, Ilan 15, and Manu 10, a golden lab named Benjy, two rats, and three cats.

Introduction

The few farm animals I encountered growing up always struck me as similar to our beloved dogs and cats. But I noticed that they were not treated with the same love and respect. In fact, I later learned that farm animals are among the most mistreated animals on the planet. What is even more heartbreaking is that these sentient creatures are acutely aware of their horrific plight. With this in mind, I visited ten farm animal sanctuaries, all passionately dedicated to the rescue, rehabilitation, and lifelong care of abused and neglected farm animals. At the sanctuaries the animals can finally live in peace. They receive love and care, and for many it is the first kindness they have experienced in their entire lives. While spending time with the animals, I confirmed what I knew in my heart to be true: they are unique individuals, with emotions and characteristics as diverse as any human. I chose to make portraits of the animals to show their personalities and to depict them in the dignified manner they deserve. The animals you see within these pages are the fortunate ones. They have been rescued from misery and torture, but startlingly, an estimated ten billion others each year will not escape. With unbelievably few laws protecting them, these living, feeling beings are forced to live in tiny confinement crates, mutilated, mistreated, and deprived of even the most basic necessities. The animals I photographed are now thriving, but upon closer inspection, you can see evidence of their traumatic pasts. For example, you might notice a duck with a missing wing that was amputated after being kicked, or an unusually small older cow, her growth stunted by starvation. What surprised and continues to amaze me is that despite the horrible cruelty these animals have endured, their spirits are unbroken.

My process for making these photographs was to sit and wait for the animals to approach me. Once they did, I was greeted in a variety of ways. Memorably, Amelia the turkey nuzzled my neck and gave me a "hug", and Dee Dee the donkey rubbed her face on my cheek and rested her head on my shoulder. I saw first-hand just how wrong the stereotypes about farm animals are. I met many intelligent pigs (they are widely considered to be the fourth smartest animal on the planet), and exceptionally clean ones at that. I witnessed strong bonds between mother and child and deep friendships between unlikely pairs, such as Barbie the hen and Rambo the ram who were snuggling together when I visited Catskill Sanctuary. Each portrait of a safe, rescued farm animal is a plea to help those who are still suffering, and to see farm animals as the remarkable, emotional beings they truly are. I invite you to view these photographs with a compassionate eye and to read their stories with an open heart. My hope is that you will begin to see farm animals in a new light.

Sharon Lee Hart

Sharon Lee Hart was born in Washington, DC and teaches photography at the University of Kentucky. She lives in Lexington, KY with her partner Izel, two happy, chatty cats, Finnie and Maxwell, and a house full of succulents. Hart earned her MFA from the University of North Carolina at Chapel Hill and her BFA from Maine College of Art. A vegetarian for over 20 years, Hart became vegan after spending time with the amazing animals she met while working on her "Farm Animal Sanctuary" project. She recently received a grant from the Tennessee State Art Commission and an activist award for her "Sanctuary" project from PhotoPhilanthropy. She has exhibited her photographs and mixed media works throughout the country. Her work can be viewed by visiting sharonleehart.com and farmanimalsanctuaryproject.com

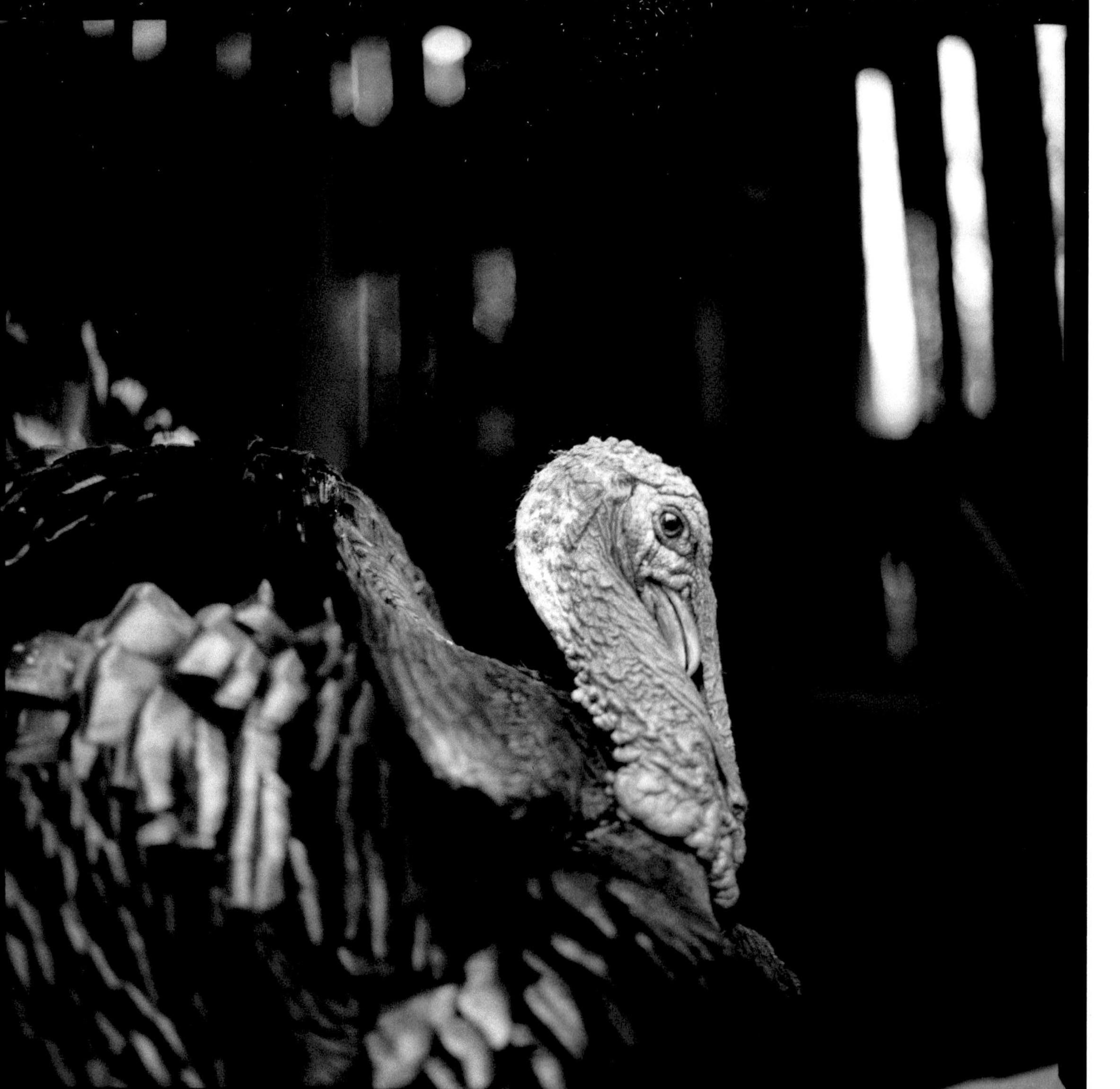

Victor

Victor was found walking down a sidewalk in Germantown, MD on Thanksgiving Day 2005. He was taken by Animal Control to a local wildlife rehabilitator, as they thought he was a wild turkey. When he started following the staff around the facility, they realized he was a tame domestic bird, and brought him to Poplar Spring, where he has lived happily ever since. His favorite girl turkey is Gertrude, who was found in a cage behind a restaurant.

Victor loves to strut around all puffed up and displaying constantly, showing off for human visitors and turkeys alike.

Terry Cummings
Co-Founder
Poplar Spring Animal Sanctuary

Dee Dee Donkey

Dee Dee Donkey is a miniature Sicillian, and is approximately 33 year old. She was taken in by Days End Farm Horse Rescue along with some ponies and horses who had been locked up in a barn for an indeterminate amount of time. Dee Dee had a hard adjustment period at first, and is still claustrophobic in closed stalls, but she *loves* people, most especially children. She likes to lean on people and sometimes will try to sit on their laps.

Her job is to chase off strange animals from the field – to keep the sheep and goats safe, and to sound the alarm with her braying if anything is amiss. She does this very well despite her age and somewhat overweight condition. Dee Dee's special friend is Bello the Dutch Warmblood horse. She also has an on-again, off-again romance with Jean-Claude the llama.

\- Farmer Anne, Star Gazing Farm

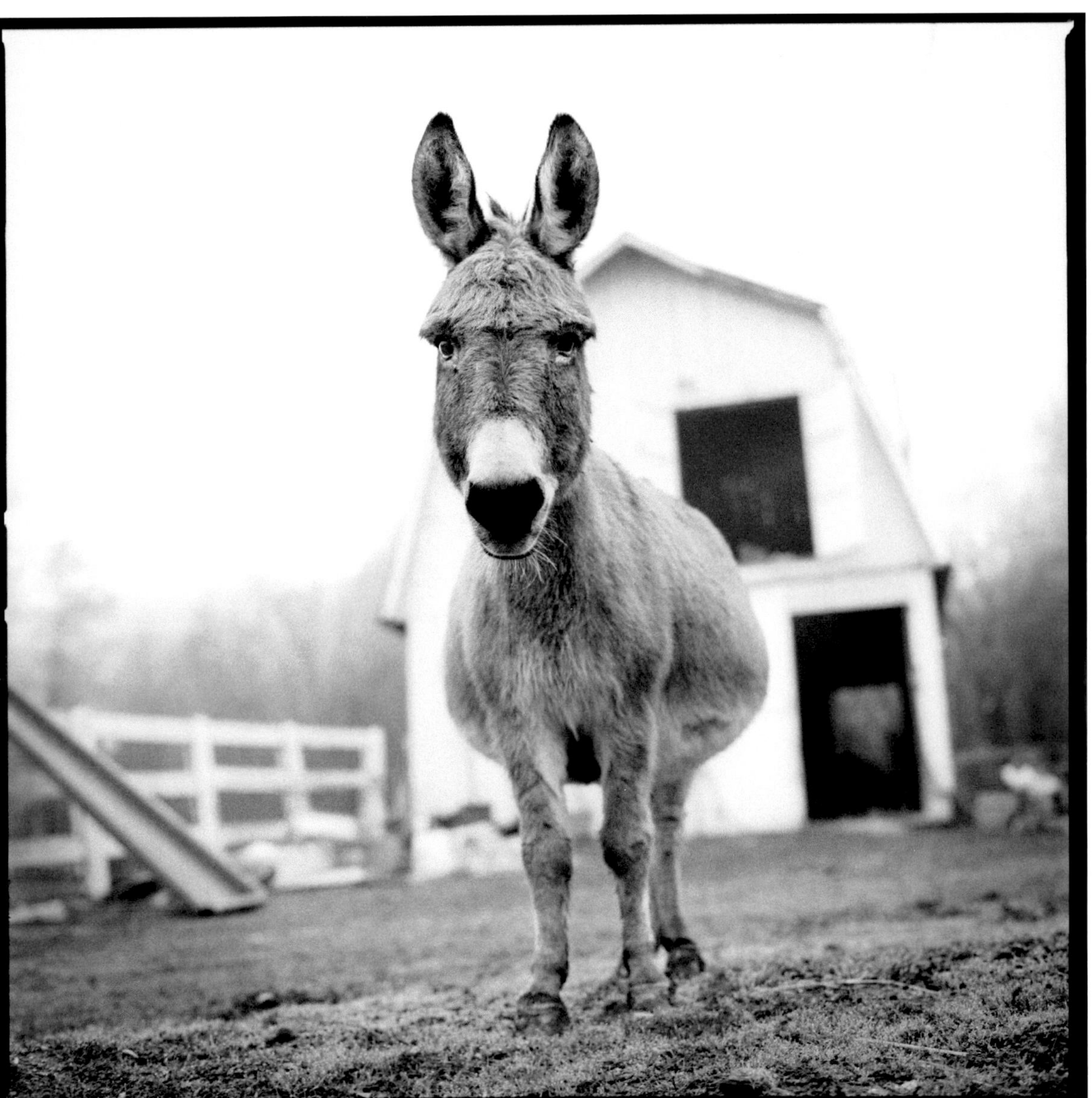

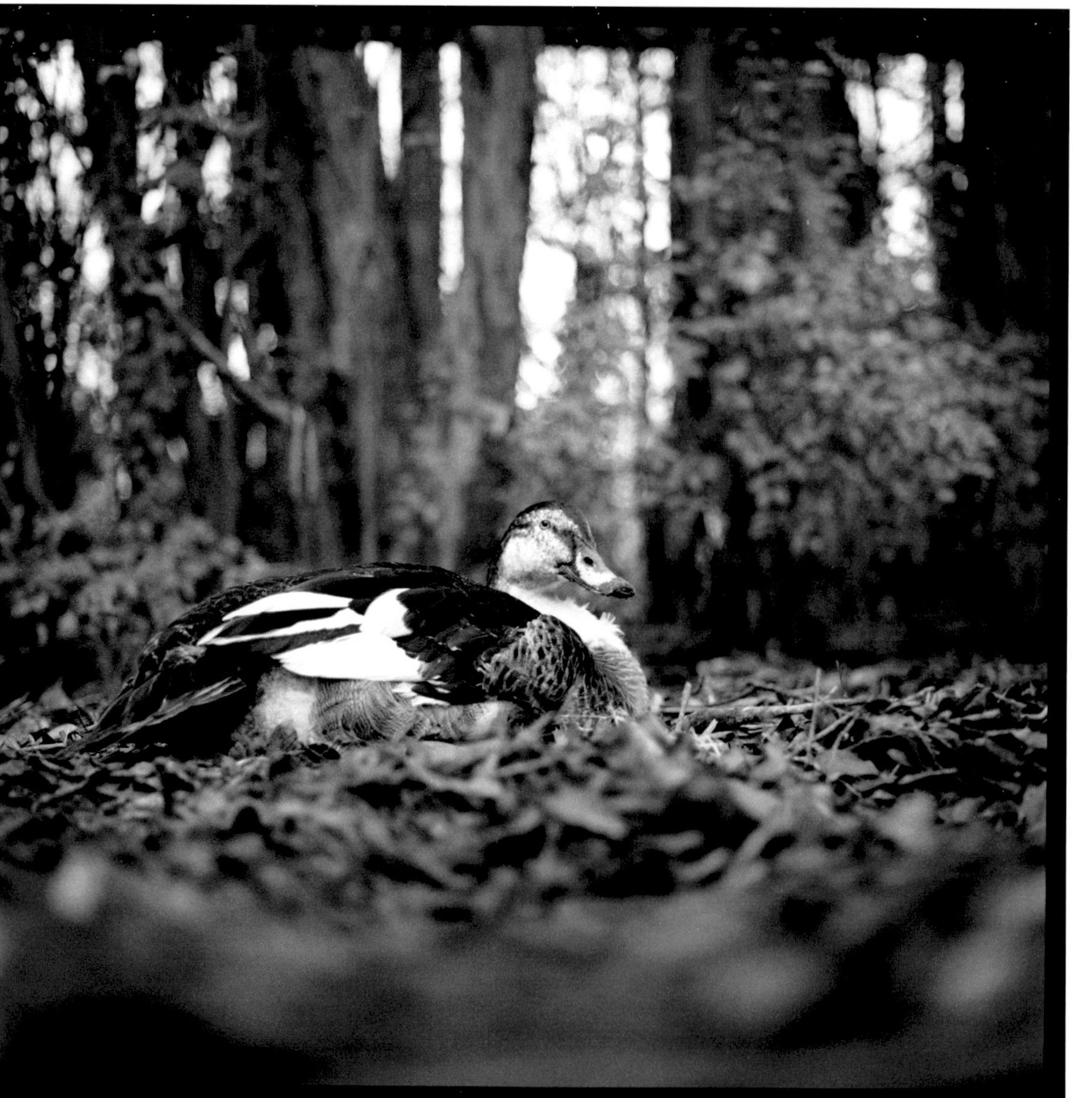

ARNOLD

Arnold was rescued from Hudson Valley Foie Gras, in upstate New York. He was brought to our sanctuary with his companion, Donald, who has since passed away. From the time Arnold and Donald arrived they were inseparable, plodding about the sanctuary together, swimming and splashing in their blue plastic pool, and expressing their happiness with loud and quiet quacking.

Arnold loves padding about in the woods with the chickens. And he loves spaghetti. When I bring out a pan of his favorite pasta, Arnold is on the spot, digging in. Though Donald is no longer with him, Arnold shares his days contentedly with the chickens and our elderly white Pekin duck, Terrain. I should ~~add~~ that all of our birds love spaghetti!

Karen Davis, Founder
United Poultry Concerns

Drew

Drew was found wandering a Chicago-area cemetery. According to the compassionate folks who convinced him to ride with them all the way to Michigan, finding roosters, dead or alive, is not entirely unheard of in the area, where certain religious followers believe that roosters are symbols of watchfulness, courage and vigilance and will watch over their departed loved ones. Whatever the reason for his abandonment in the cemetery, we're glad he was rescued before he faced a windy, cold Chicago winter.

Amanda
SASHA Farm

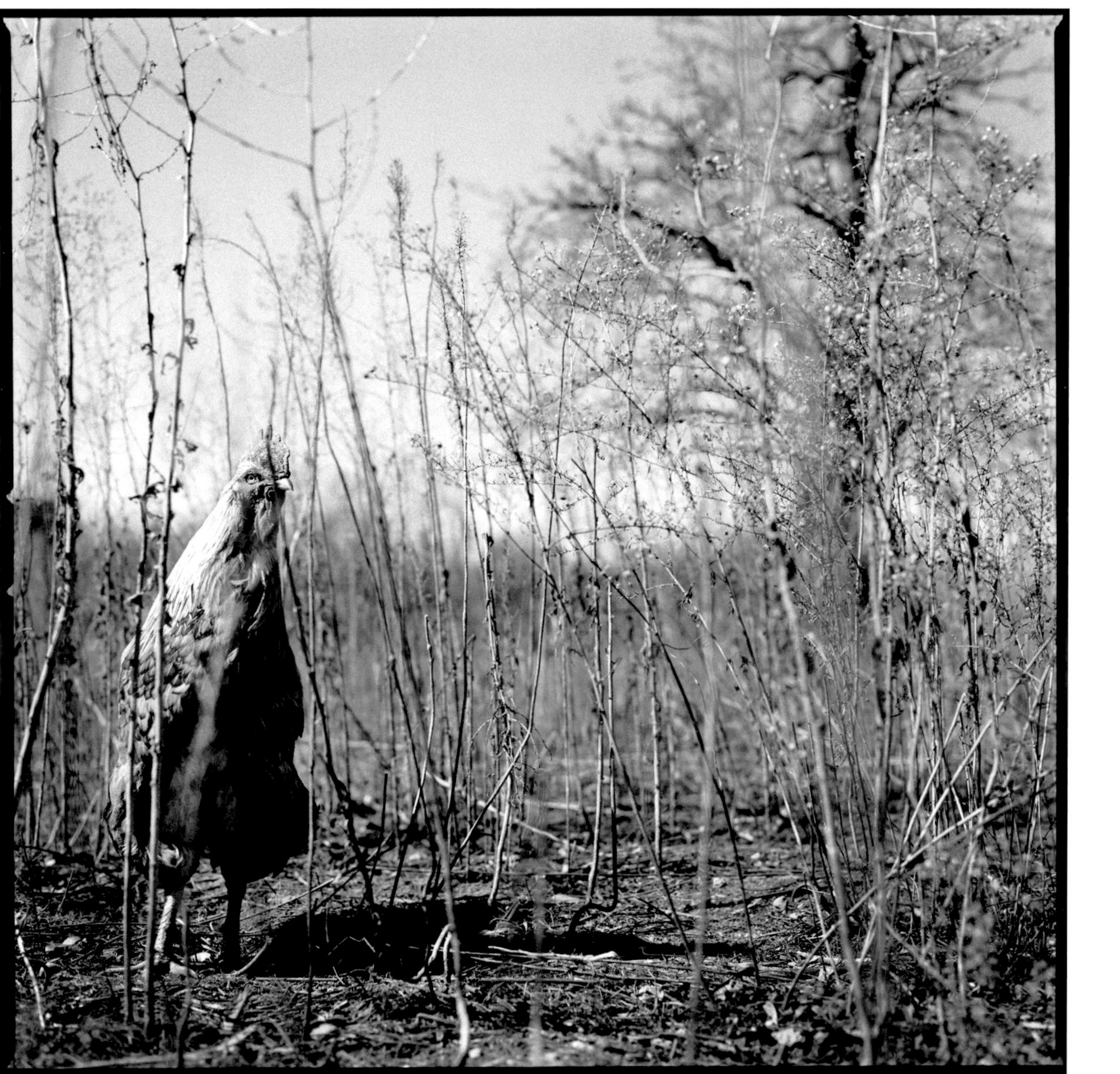

Lil' Jay

One of the luckiest goats at Woodstock Farm Animal Sanctuary, Lil' Jay was born at a goat farm where the farmer had a change of heart and no longer wanted to exploit and harm them. Lil' Jay, along with many other goats, was rescued and brought to another sanctuary in Pennsylvania. When the sanctuary unfortunately closed in 2005, Lil' Jay and all of his goat and sheep friends came to live at the Woodstock Farm Animal Sanctuary. He settled in quickly and became part of the big goat gang with Gilbert, Houdini, Madison and Victor. Lil' Jay was very sweet with people and liked to hang out on the rock pile with his friends! Sadly, he passed away this year after fighting an illness for several months. While Lil' Jay is missed, we are comforted in knowing that he was spared the suffering that so many goats endure and was able to live his life in peace among friends at the sanctuary.

~ Jenny Brown and Doug Abel
Co-Founders
Woodstock Farm Animal Sanctuary

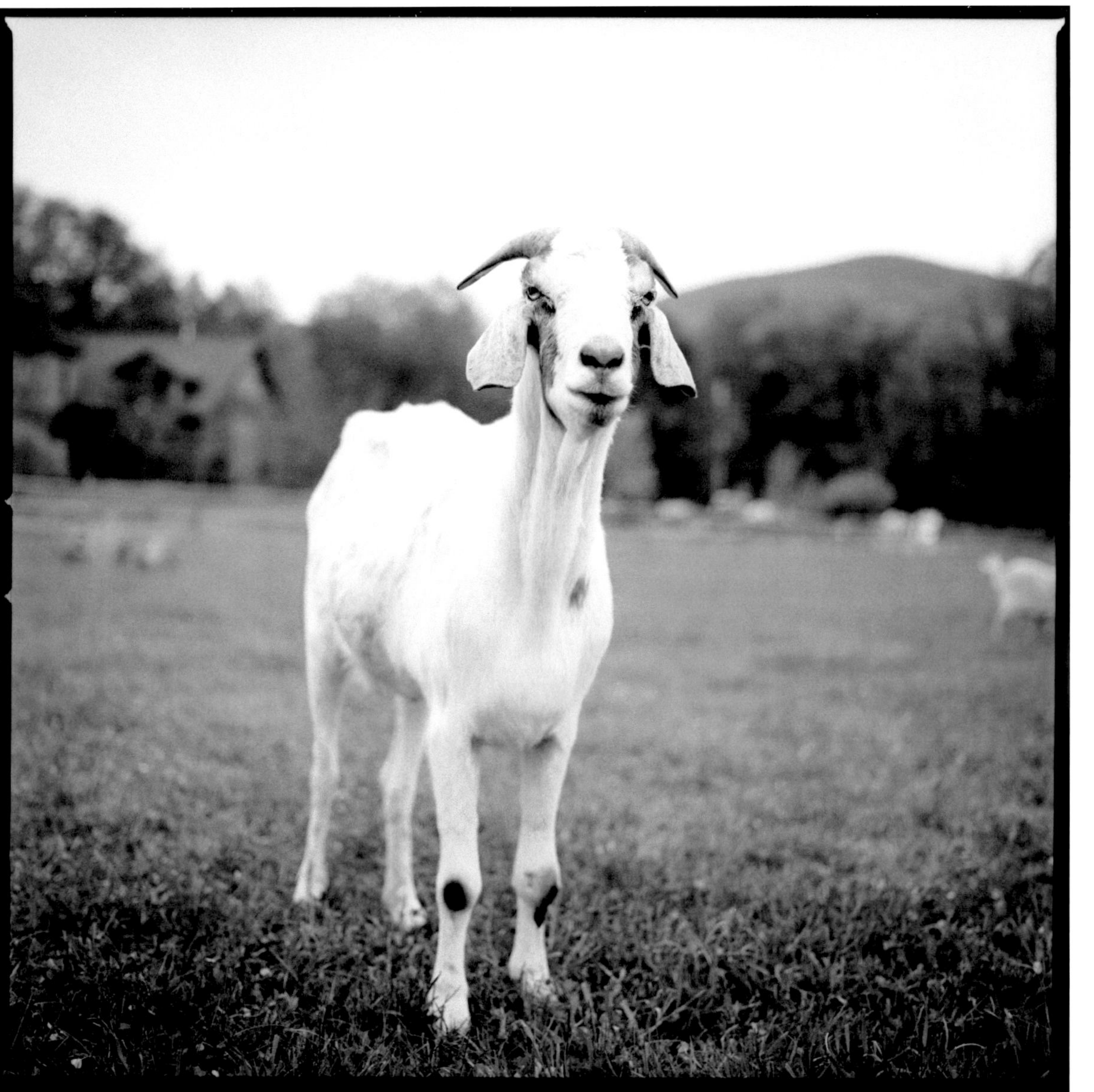

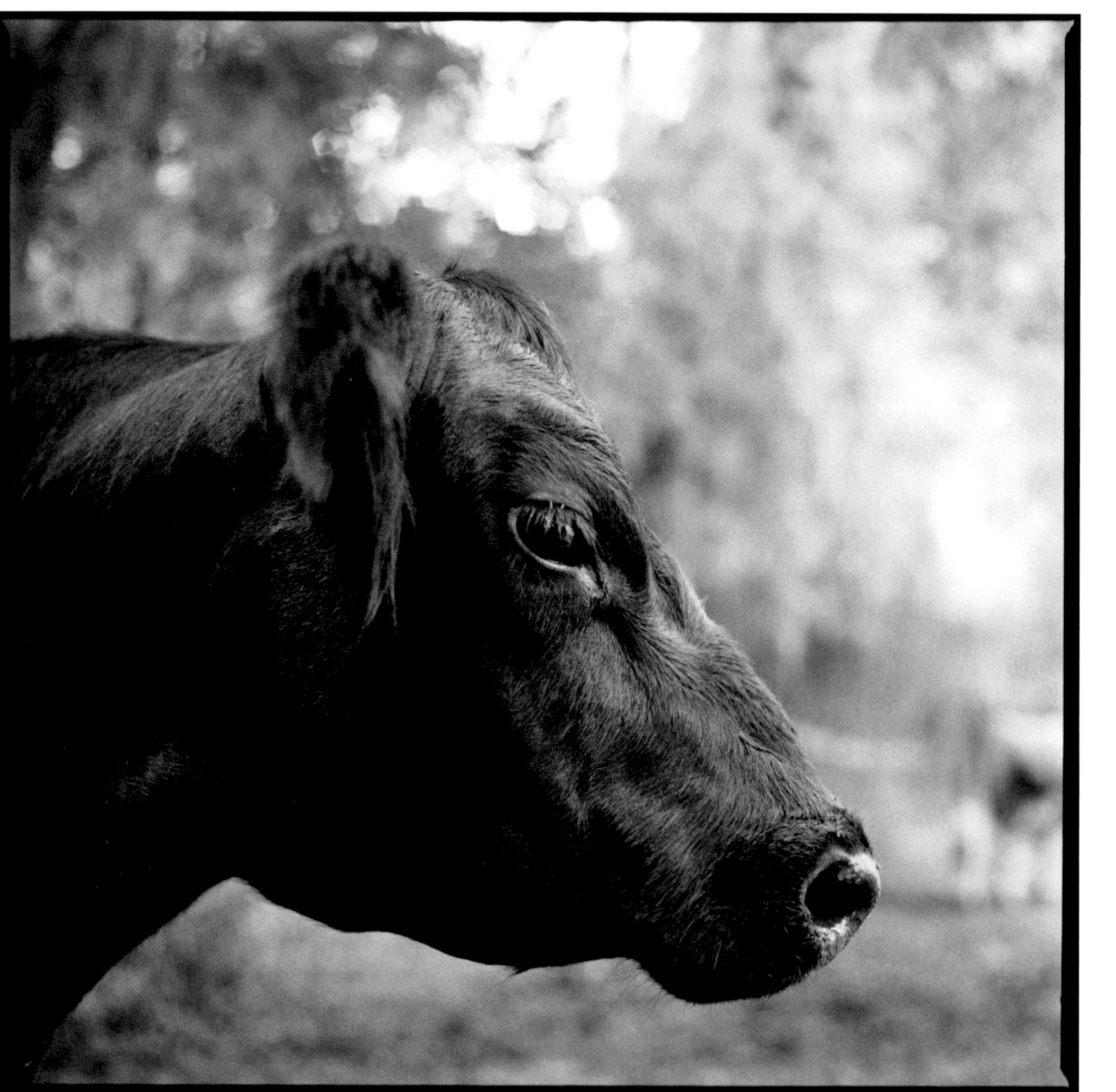

Betty

Betty was left to starve in a field, along with her herd mates, Panda, Aggie and Aggie's baby Shelby. All four of these girls were very under weight when they arrived at the sanctuary in 2008.

Betty and her friends have all made full recoveries and now spend their days grazing, napping in the shade and making friends with our volunteers.

Aimee Pritchard
Kindred Spirits Sanctuary

Russell

Russell is a handsome rooster who was discovered strolling across a very busy intersection on Connecticut Ave. in the heart of Washington D.C. Residents of a nearby apartment building were able to catch him and bring him to the sanctuary, naming him Russell Crow. He is very charming and is the head rooster in his group, with many girlfriend hens. He watches over his girls, calling out an alarm call so they can run to safety if he sees any predators, and he finds food for them, clucking excitedly while they come running to peck at the treat.

Terry Cummings
Co-Founder
Poplar Spring Animal Sanctuary

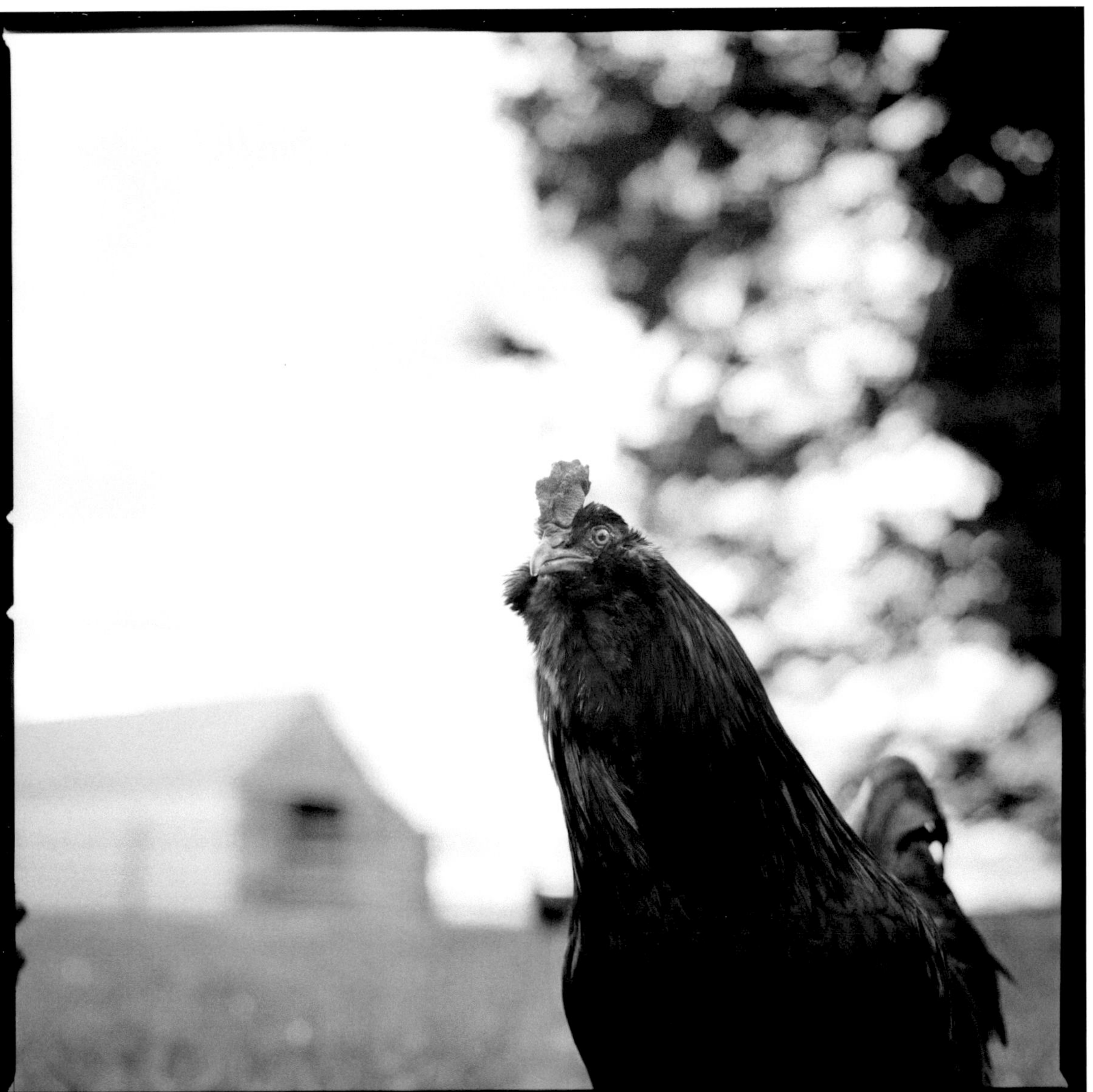

Aintcho

Aintcho Cow found his forever home at the sanctuary all on his own.

In 2004, florida was hit by several large hurricanes. After each storm staff of the sanctuary walks the grounds to check on everyone and to do a head count.

After one of the storms staff noticed two extra cows in the cow yard. There were no farms near by so Aintcho and his friend Nacho must have trecked quite a way through the storm to find their perfect home.

Today Aintcho has his own herd to look after, and has never made any attempts to leave.

Logan Vindett
Kindred Spirits Sanctuary

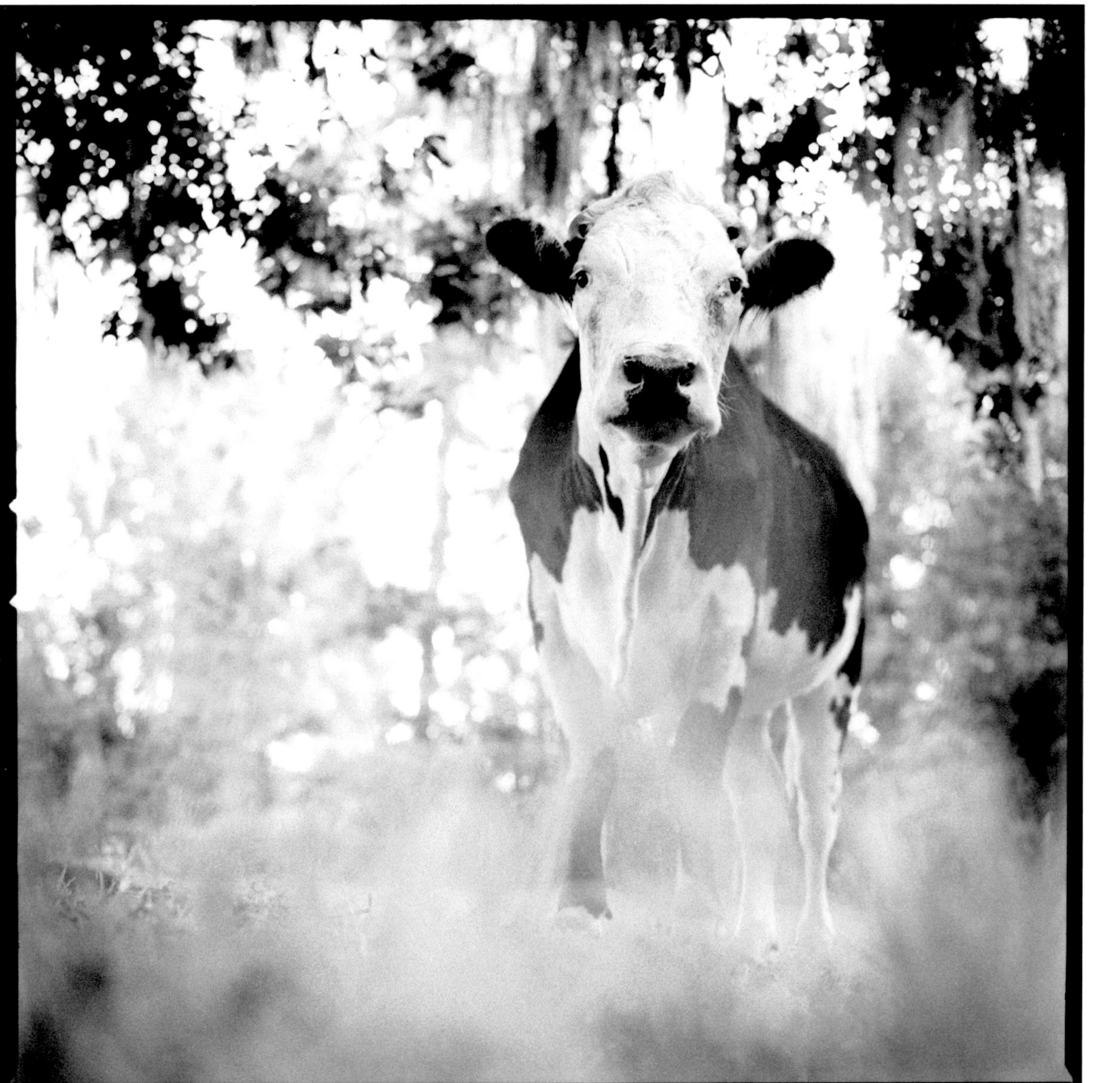

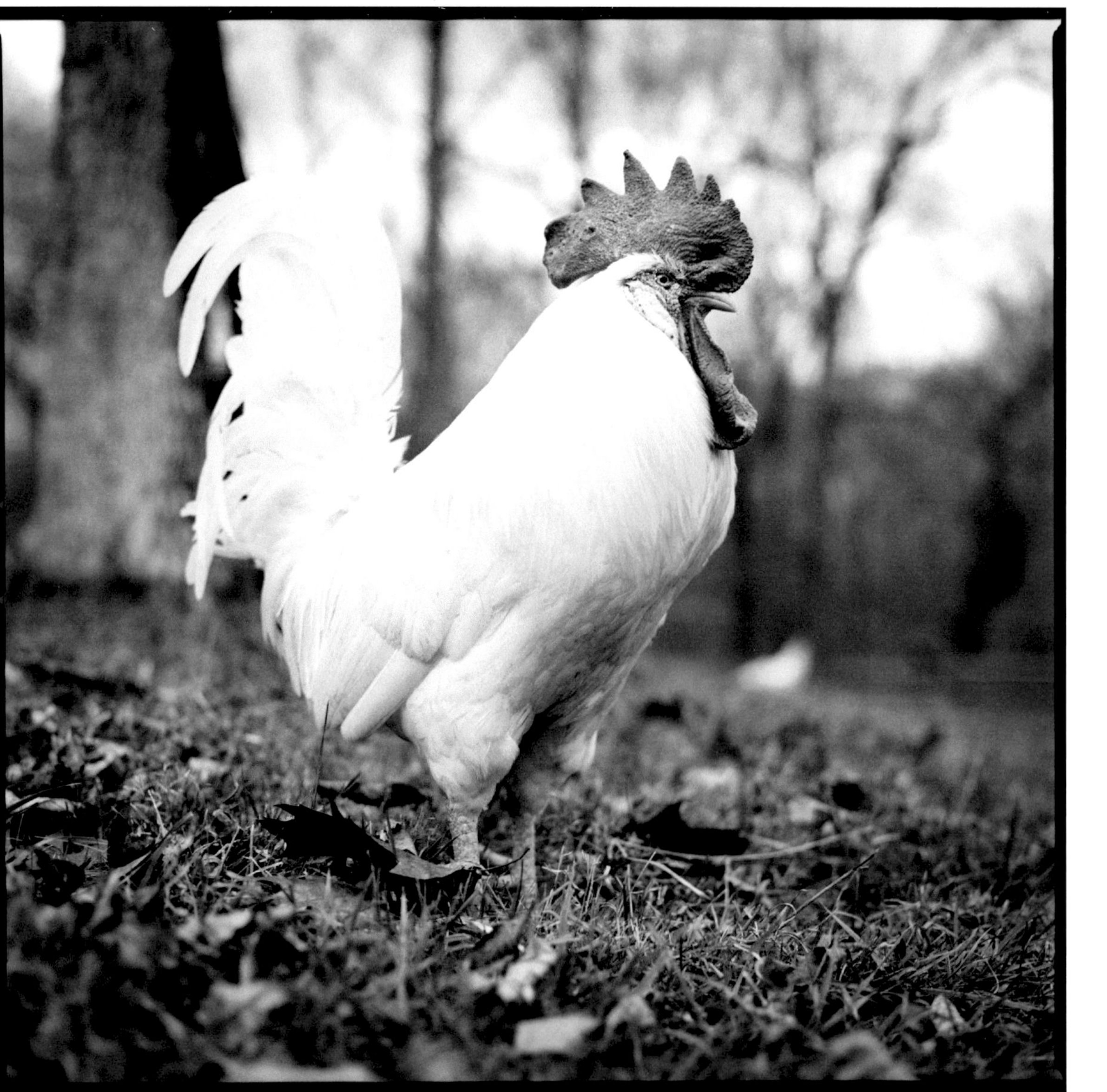

Hermie

Hermie was just a tiny chick when he arrived at Poplar Spring, an adorable fuzzy little peeping baby. He was rescued by a young girl from a reptile show, where he was being sold for snake food. We kept him in a playpen in the kitchen with a heat lamp to keep him warm, and a teddy bear that he slept underneath like a mother hen. He quickly grew into a handsome white Leghorn rooster, who loves to crow all day long, and enjoys being held and petted.

Terry Cummings
Co-Founder
Poplar Spring Animal Sanctuary

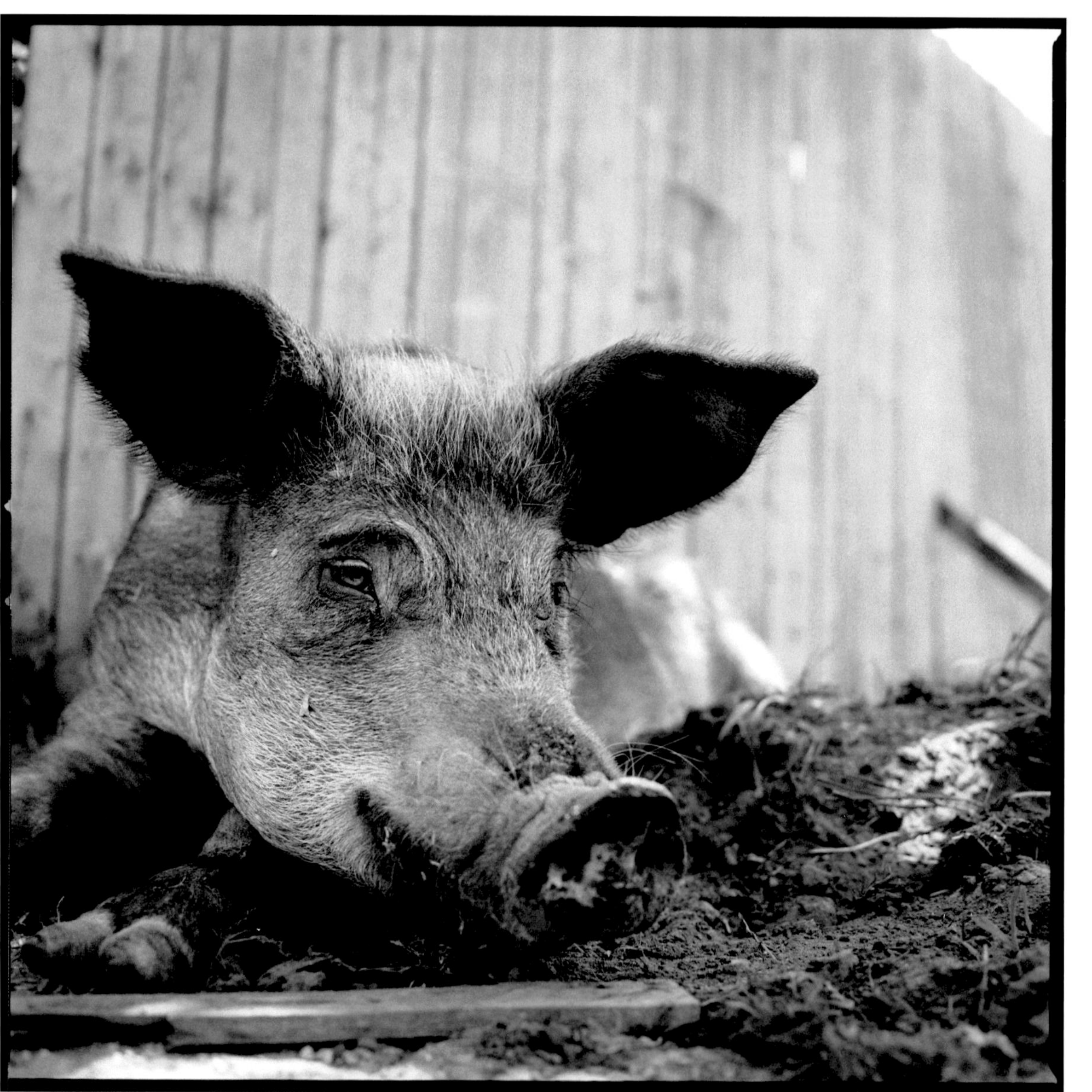

Mary Jane

She came to us at Christmas, extremely runty and sick and tiny like a guinea pig. Had been abandoned at the Amish farm she was born at. Someone bought her for 7$ and brought her here. She leaked diarrhea constantly for days - she was so pitiful. Eventually got well and moved outside - then a strangulated hernia in her belly. $500.00 vet bill for her operation. Since then, she has done well except for an injury when a cow stepped on her. She keeps plugging along! Very sweet and girly - we adore Mary Jane.

- Shannon Sheridan,
Grateful Acres Sanctuary

Duncan

In 2009 Duncan and another young goat, Isadora, were spotted along side of the Hutchinson River Parkway in the Bronx. Because of their shifty moves, it took the animal control authorities two days to capture them. The authorities suspected that the goats had escaped a live meat market.

Duncan and Isadora were initially sent to the Farm Sanctuary in Watkins Glen, New York, for medical evaluation and treatment. After three months, the Farm Sanctuary sent the two goats to us for their permanent home.

When Duncan arrived, the other goats and sheep put him in his place, forcing him to stay in his own part of the pasture. Isadora always joined Duncan. But after his first winter on the farm, Duncan emerged strong and forceful. He began butting heads with everyone and became the most playful animal on our farm.

Duncan loves to run, jump and explore. He sneaks into chicken aviaries, jumps on wheel barrows and steals gloves from people's pockets. In the morning, when the other animals are running into the pasture for their hay, Duncan sometimes lingers in the barn, seeing what he can find to play with. He'd rather play than eat.

Bill and Ellen Crain
Founders,
Safe Haven Farm Sanctuary

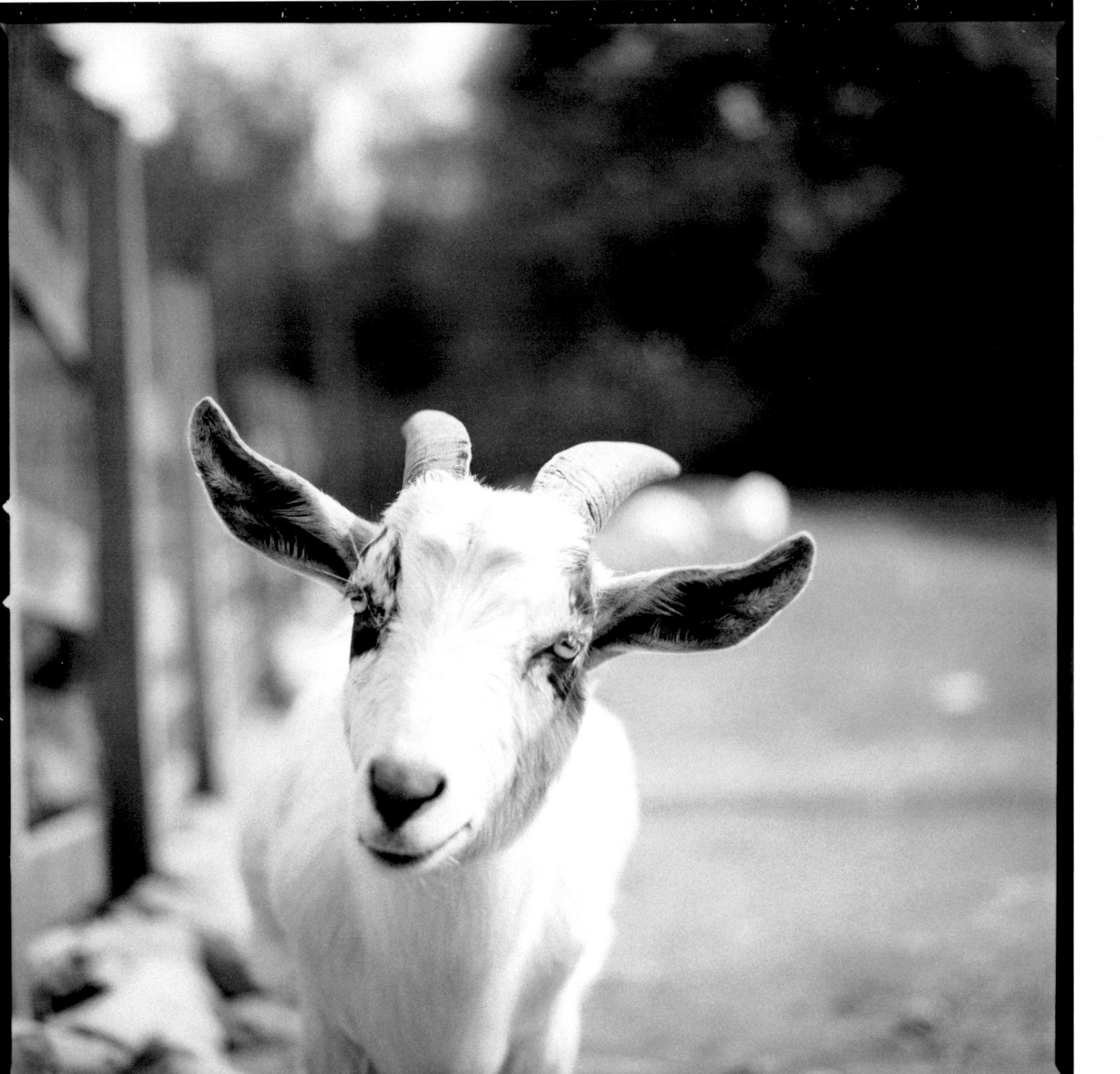

Meg

Left without food or water in a filthy, overcrowded barn, Meg and dozens of other cows and calves were injured, emaciated and standing in three feet of manure when rescuers found them in March 2004. Many animals on the Pennsylvania property had already died of neglect. The survivors, including Meg, were confiscated by the local humane society and brought to safety at our New York shelter. Here, Meg recovered her health and discovered a happiness she had never before known. During her time with us this sweet cow has become a mother figure to many a newly rescued calf, and now 10 year old, she is enjoying her golden years among her many friends in our cattle herd, wandering our lush pastures without a care in the world.

Gene Baur, Farm Sanctuary

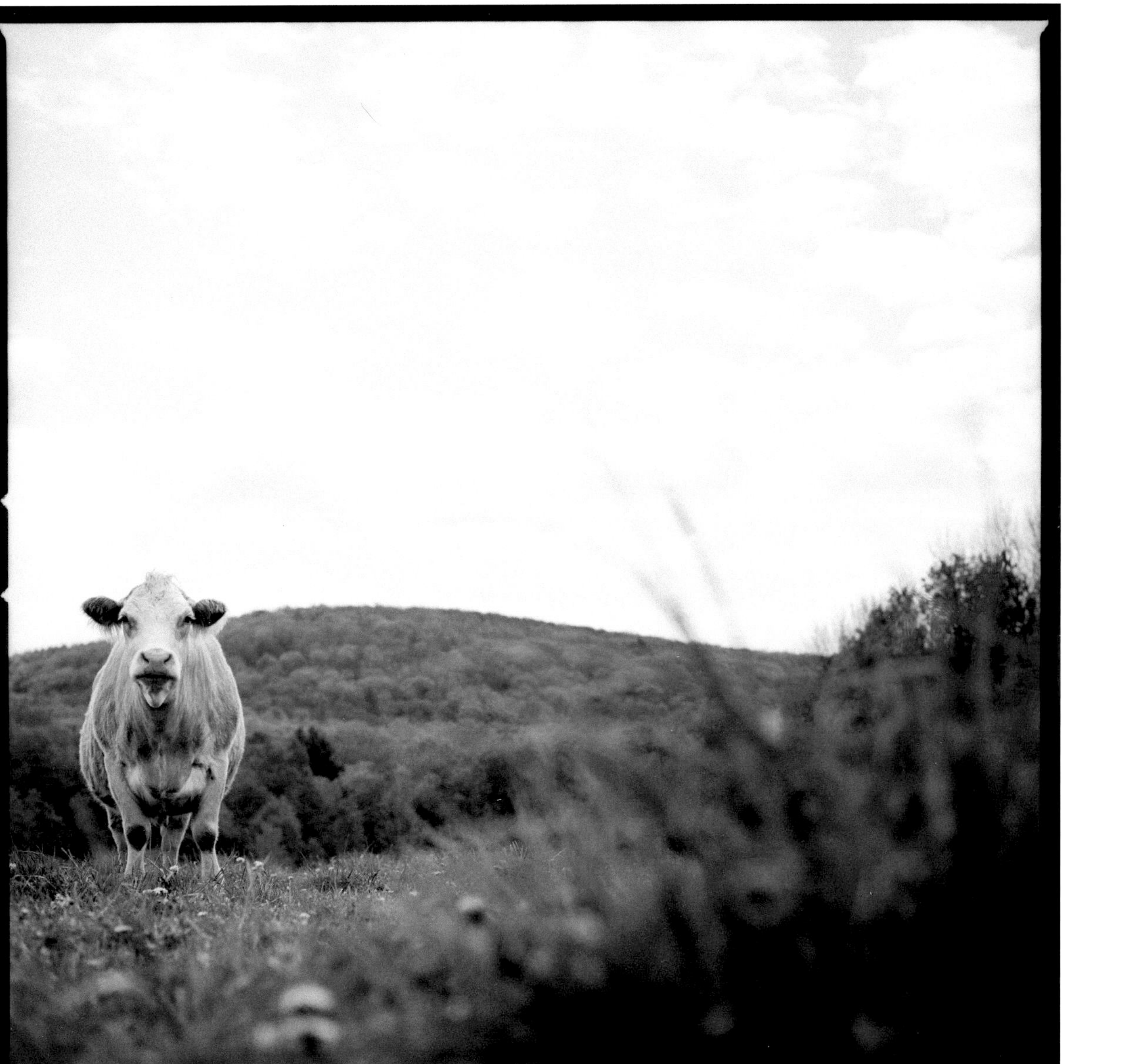

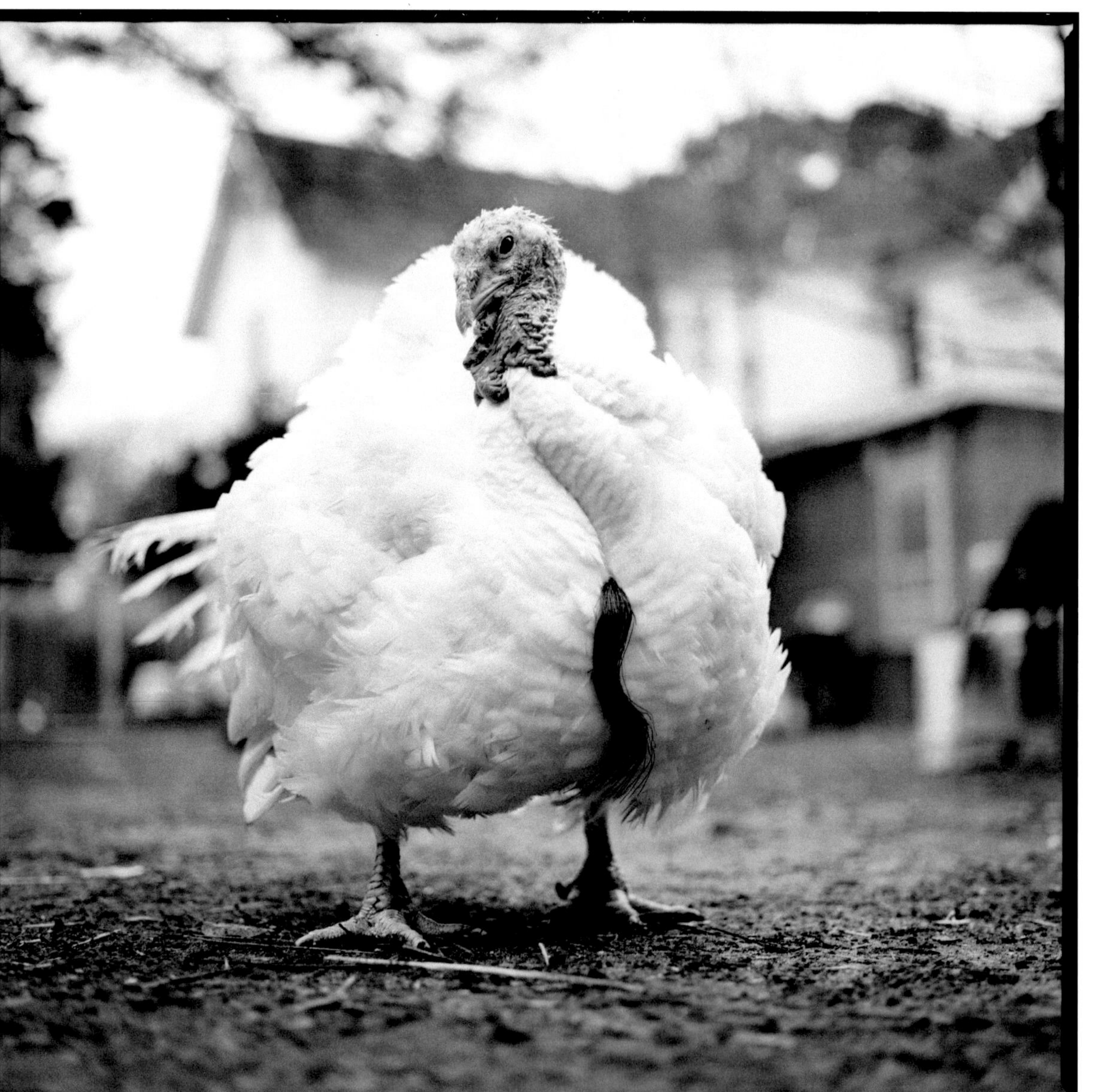

Amelia

We adopted Amelia in the fall of 2007. A local farmer gave her up as "too expensive" to keep. Amelia has lived happily in our sanctuary ever since. She hangs out with the chickens, sits with them under the trees in the afternoon sunlight, and when people visit, Amelia fans out her snow white tail feathers, just like a male turkey, and joins the visitors in a stroll through the sanctuary yard, never leaving their side. Amelia chose a leafy nesting place to quietly lay her eggs. In the evening she stays outside with the ducks until the very last minute, but when I call to her, "Come on Amelia, time for bed," she slowly makes her way into her house, following her duck friends, for the night.

Karen Davis, founder
United Poultry Concerns

Jesse

Jesse came to the Sanctuary with his best pal Sonny. Sonny was sick with a terminal illness. Jesse stuck right by his friends side until the end.

Jesse now lives with our other horses and burros, but spends must of his time with his good friend Cora. Jesse loves to watch as we complete morning Chores and he is always there when you need some one to talk to.

Logan Undett
Kindred Spirits Sanctuary

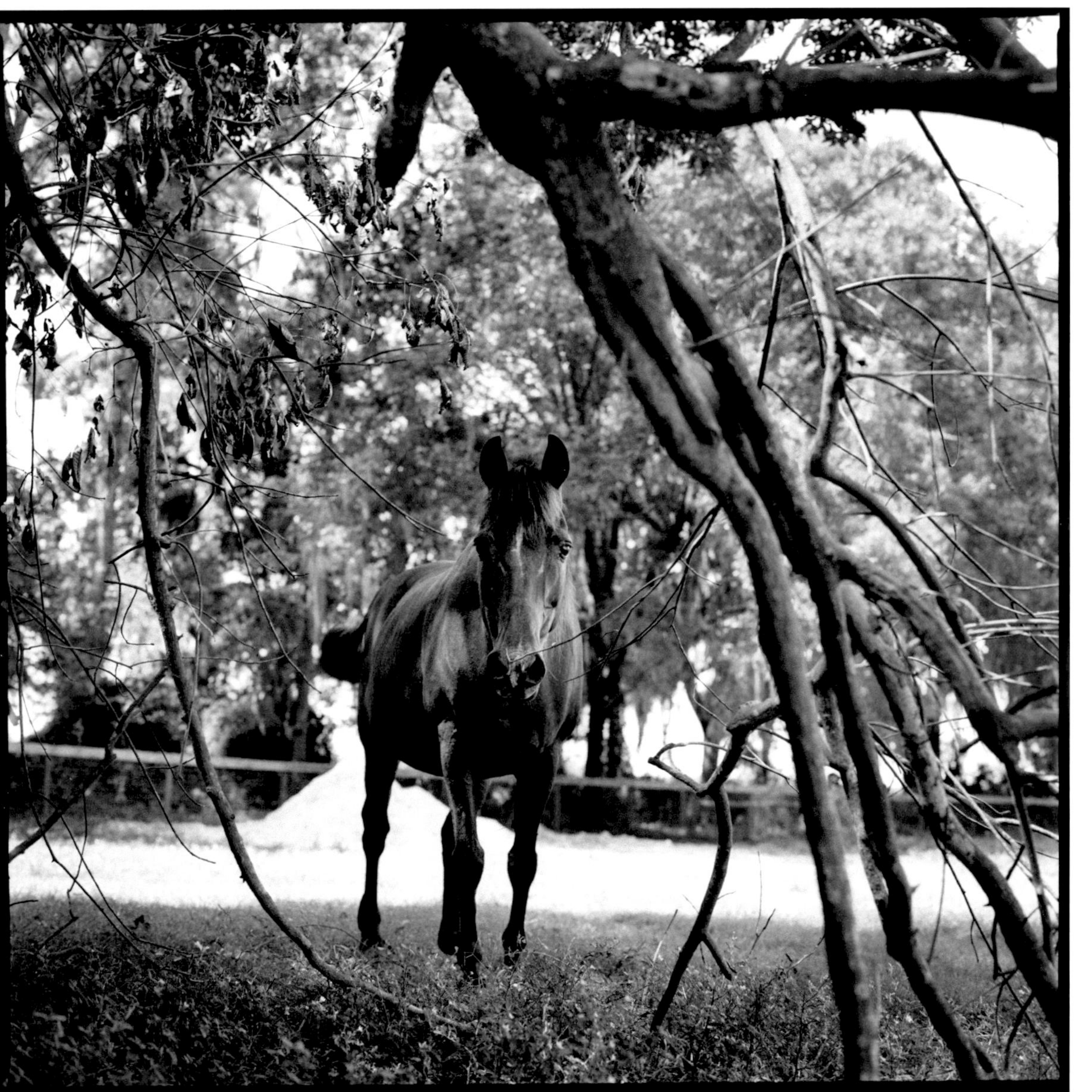

Farm Sanctuary

Gene Bauer

In the summer of 1986, I met the sheep who would change everything. I had been investigating Lancaster Stockyards, a sprawling Pennsylvania auction facility where hordes of frightened, exhausted animals were driven from trucks to be sold for fattening or slaughter. Many never made it to the auction floor. Those who died from the hardships of their lives on the farm, or from the harrowing journey to the yards, were dumped in a heap, called simply "the dead pile", to await the renderer. One sweltering day in August, as my partner and I approached that dumping ground, we saw a young sheep. Lying among carcasses that seethed with maggots, she appeared lifeless. But sensing someone nearby, she suddenly mustered the strength to lift her head. We knew immediately that we had to help her. In that moment, I was transformed from a witness into a rescuer.

Though we had little hope that the sheep would survive, we lifted her carefully into our van and drove the streets of Lancaster until we found a veterinarian. As he gently examined our rescue, she began to perk up, and within 20 minutes she was eating and drinking, come fully to life before our eyes. Hilda, as we later named her, was not suffering from any injuries or diseases. She had simply collapsed from the brutal conditions of her transport to the stockyard. Someone had chosen to abandon her to a slow death, though she needed only a little care and nourishment to revive. There were others like her, others we could save. And we could fight for the multitudes beyond the reach of direct rescue; laboring toward an end to the cruelty they endured in factory farms, stockyards and slaughterhouses. As Hilda found her legs, so did Farm Sanctuary.

We launched an investigation of Lancaster Stockyards, and in 1993 our prosecution of the facility resulted in the first U.S. conviction of a stockyard for mistreating a downed animal. This landmark victory of our *No Downers* campaign was followed by another two years later when we helped to pass a law in California, since emulated by other states, that prevents dragging, pushing, holding, or selling downed animals at stockyards and slaughterhouses. In 2009 the USDA finally announced a rule to prohibit the slaughter of downed cattle. While lauding this step, we continue to fight for the downed pigs, goats and sheep that still suffer horrific cruelty when they become downed at facilities throughout the country.

Meanwhile, through our *Anti-Confinement Campaign*, we have worked extensively to abolish the industry's three most torturous confinement systems: battery cages for laying hens, gestation crates for sows, and veal crates. From 2002–08, ballot initiatives backed by Farm Sanctuary achieved anti-confinement measures in Florida, Arizona and California, engendering a trend. Legislation banning one or more confinement systems has now been passed in Oregon, Colorado, Maine, and Michigan as well. In the summer of 2011, with Farm Sanctuary and other groups mustering to engage the egg industry in Oregon and Washington, the United Egg Producers agreed to support federal legislation to improve the welfare of all U.S. laying hens and eventually outlaw battery cages entirely. Industry acquiescence with this legislation testifies to the tremendous influence that Farm Sanctuary, and the farm animal protection movement as a whole, has gained over the past 25 years.

Hilda, who grew into a beautiful, healthy sheep, lived with us for 11 years. Others quickly joined her. As our organization grew, cattle, goats, sheep, pigs, chickens, turkeys, ducks, and geese found refuge with us, and we cultivated the largest farm animal rescue and refuge network in North America. At the time of writing, more than 8,000 animals have received sanctuary at our internationally recognized shelters, and another 3,000 have reached permanent, loving homes through our *Farm Animal Adoption Network*. After all these years and all these rescues, the transformations of the animals we save still amaze me. They come to us starving, diseased, and terrified. Those who sought to exploit these creatures have driven them from their right selves, but they can be brought back, and they can thrive. We've seen neglected goats, at first painfully timid of humans, become confident and curious. We've seen tiny piglets, at one time barely clinging to life, grow into healthy pigs whose robust cheerfulness lifts our own spirits. We've seen former battery cage hens, who have never moved more than a step or two in their lives, learn to run. And since our very first days, we've invited those around us to see what we see, because often the most profound change begins simply with one person and one animal meeting each other.

Every year, thousands visit our shelters, many coming face-to-face with farm animals for the first time. They see that each animal is unique, with as much personality and with as great a need and a worthiness for kindness as a companion dog or cat. That shock of recognition has turned omnivores into vegans and vegans into ardent activists.

A critical function of our education program has been to catalyze such revelations, which change the manner in which individuals live and which, in aggregate, can alter the tenor of our culture. In addition to our visitor program and the conferences and celebrations that draw people to our shelters, our educational campaigns and media outreach introduce our mission to millions of people around the world. Events such as our annual *Adopt-A-Turkey Project* and *Walk for Farm Animals* galvanize thousands of participants across the country, fostering a nationwide community of advocates. Though the members of this community may be separated by thousands of miles, the animals connect us all.

The factory farming industry attempts to reduce its victims, to transform them from sentient beings into mere bodies. It does not succeed. Even in debasement, the internal lives of these animals persist. When animals have been rescued and healed, these internal lives flourish. They are themselves. And this is a restoration of agency, for simply through being themselves, these creatures, more than mere victims or beneficiaries, have the power to stir a feeling of kinship in the human heart. They have the power to change minds, and habits, and lives. They work the true transformation.

Gene Baur is the co-founder and president of Farm Sanctuary. Gene holds a master's degree in agricultural economics from Cornell University. He has conducted hundreds of visits to farms, stockyards and slaughterhouses to document conditions, and his pictures and videos, exposing factory farming cruelty, have been aired nationally and internationally, educating millions. He has testified in court and before local, state and federal legislative bodies, and has initiated groundbreaking legal enforcement and legislative action to raise awareness and prevent factory farming abuses. He played a significant role in passing the first U.S. laws to prohibit cruel farming systems, including the Florida ban on gestation crates, the Arizona ban on veal and gestation crates, and the California and Chicago bans on foie gras. His book, *Farm Sanctuary: Changing Hearts and Minds About Animals and Food*, was published by Simon and Schuster in 2008 and has become a national best seller.

Penelope

Bidders at the stockyard deemed Penelope worthless, declining to pay even $1 for the tiny calf. Penelope was a "downer," the industry term for an animal too sick, weak or injured to stand. Such animals are typically left to languish for hours or days without food or water, often thrown on "dead piles" await the renderer. Had she been purchased, Penelope likely would have been killed immediately for cheap "bob veal" or spent months tied up in a tiny crate, barely able to move, before being slaughtered for more expensive veal. Such is the fate of the many unwanted calves produced by the dairy industry as it forces its milking cows through a perpetual cycle of insemination, pregnancy and lactation that ends, after about three years, at the slaughterhouse. But Penelope was one of the very few to escape this fate. Rescued by Farm Sanctuary, she lived out her days at our New York Shelter, serenly roaming our pastures into ripe old age.

Gene Baur, Farm Sanctuary

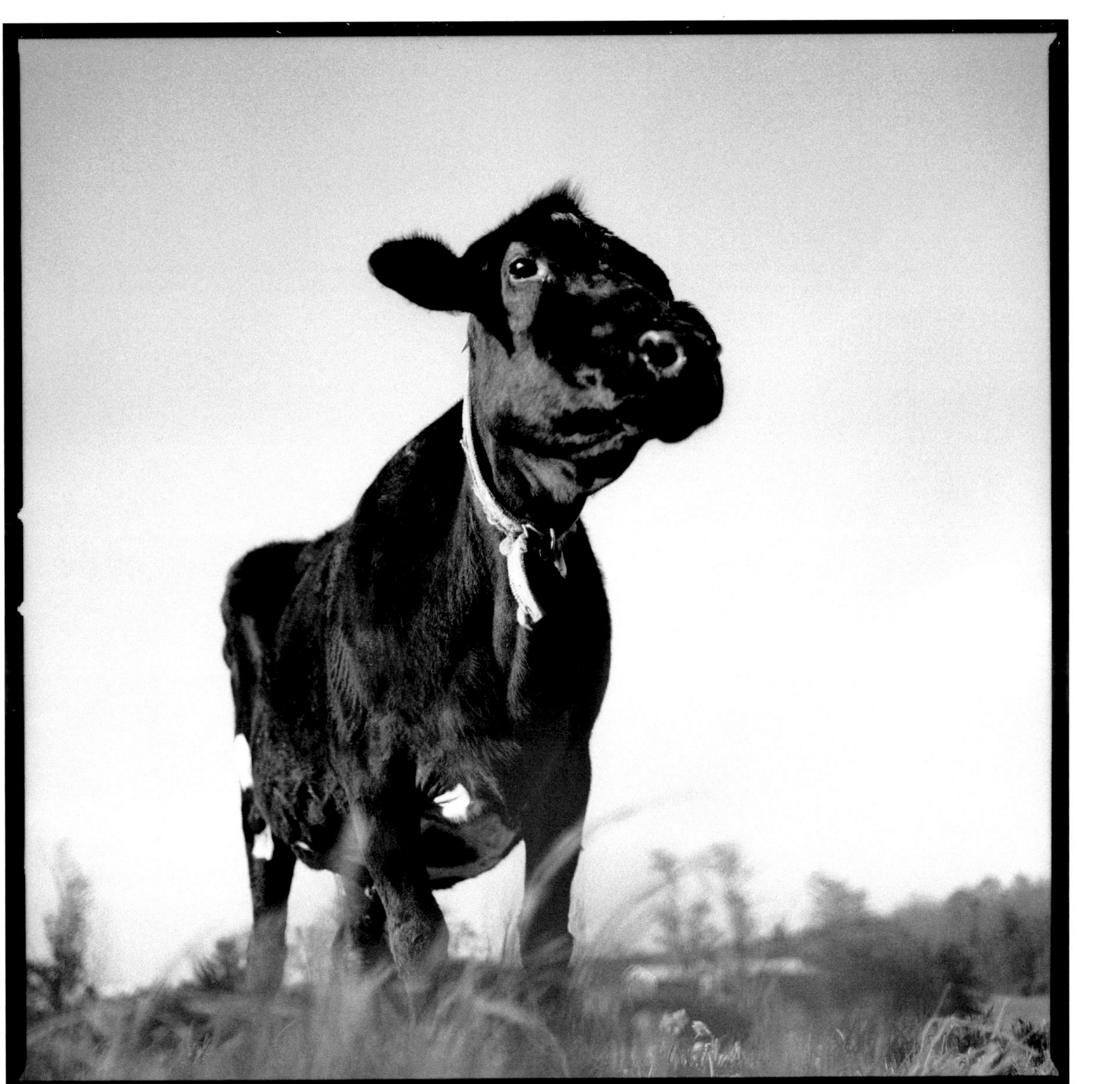

Mata Hari

By the time Mata Hari came to live at SASHA Farm, she was already a local celebrity. She'd made the news twice, bloggers were following her travels, and she even had her own Facebook fan page. She was "The Ann Arbor Sheep," an elusive ewe who had managed to evade capture for months as she grazed Ann Arbor parks and cemetaries, stopped traffic at busy intersections, interrupted business meetings and tennis matches and became to some an urban legend.

She began frequenting a secluded area behind an Art Van Furniture store, and after she seemed ready to stay awhile, they began feeding her. When she showed up one day with a badly wounded neck from a dog attack during the night, they feared she might die of infection. After the police and local animal control were unsuccessful in their attempts to catch her, employees called SASHA Farm. A pen was erected behind the building in the spot where they fed her, and the next day, the door was closed and she was on her way to her new home at SASHA Farm.

That wasn't the end, though. A month later, her wounds healed and her health restored, she surprised everyone by giving birth to twin boys. Little Art and Van still spend most of their time with their mom, even a year later.

Amanda - SASHA Farm

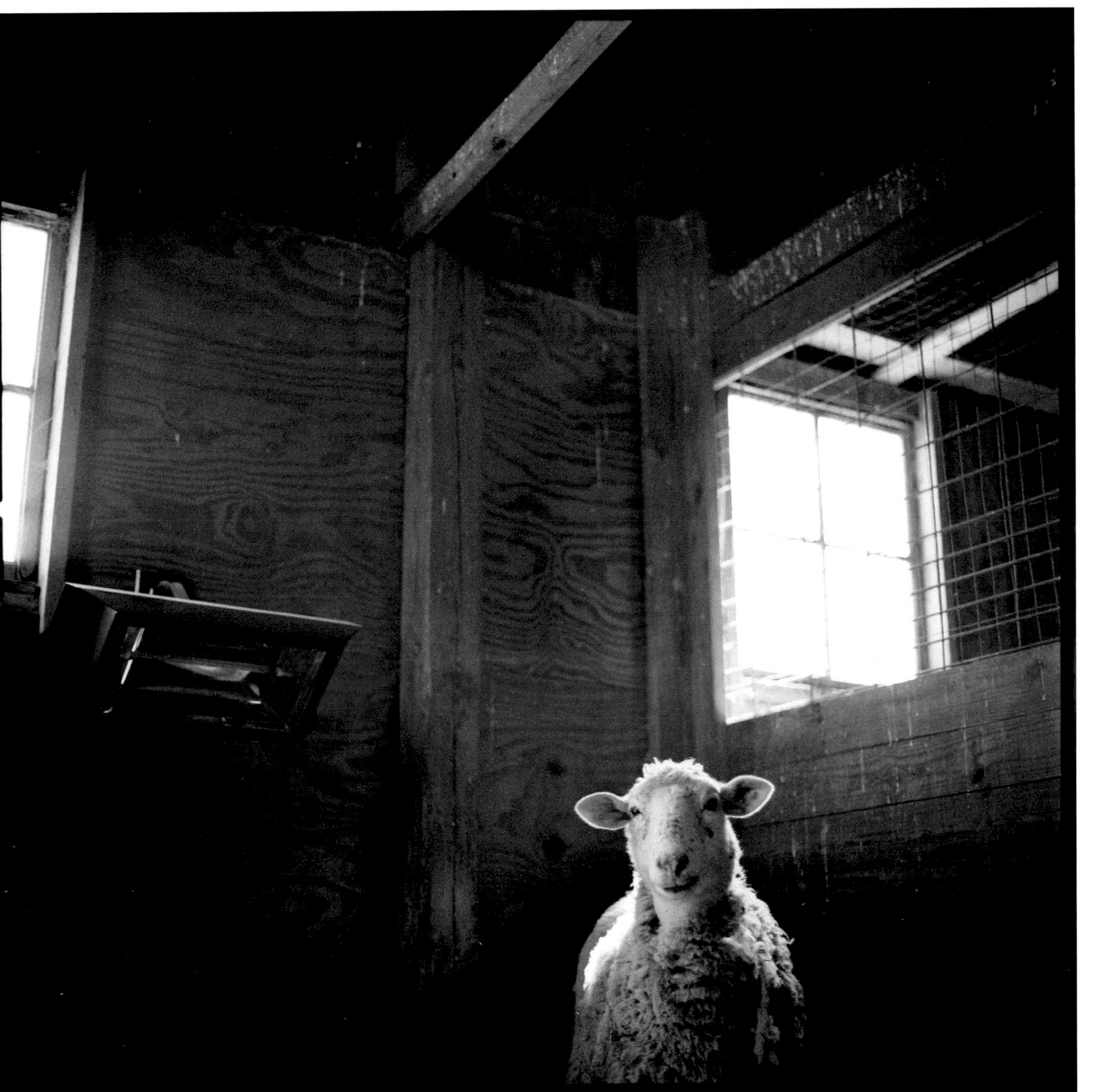

Norman

Norman was a veal calf, originally rescued as a baby from an auction by another sanctuary. He came to us as an adult with his girlfriend, a large black Angus cow named Ellie May. Norman and Ellie May were inseparable, always grazing together and sleeping side by side in the barn at night. When Ellie May passed away after many years together, Norman grieved for weeks, wandering the fields looking for her, and refusing to eat. He ever slept on top of her grave. Eventually he regained his sweet exuberant personality, but he has been a loner amongst the other cows ever since. He is a gentle giant who loves people and enjoys getting treats. His favorites are apples and cinnamon buns.

Terry Cummings Co-Founder Poplar Spring Animal Sanctuary

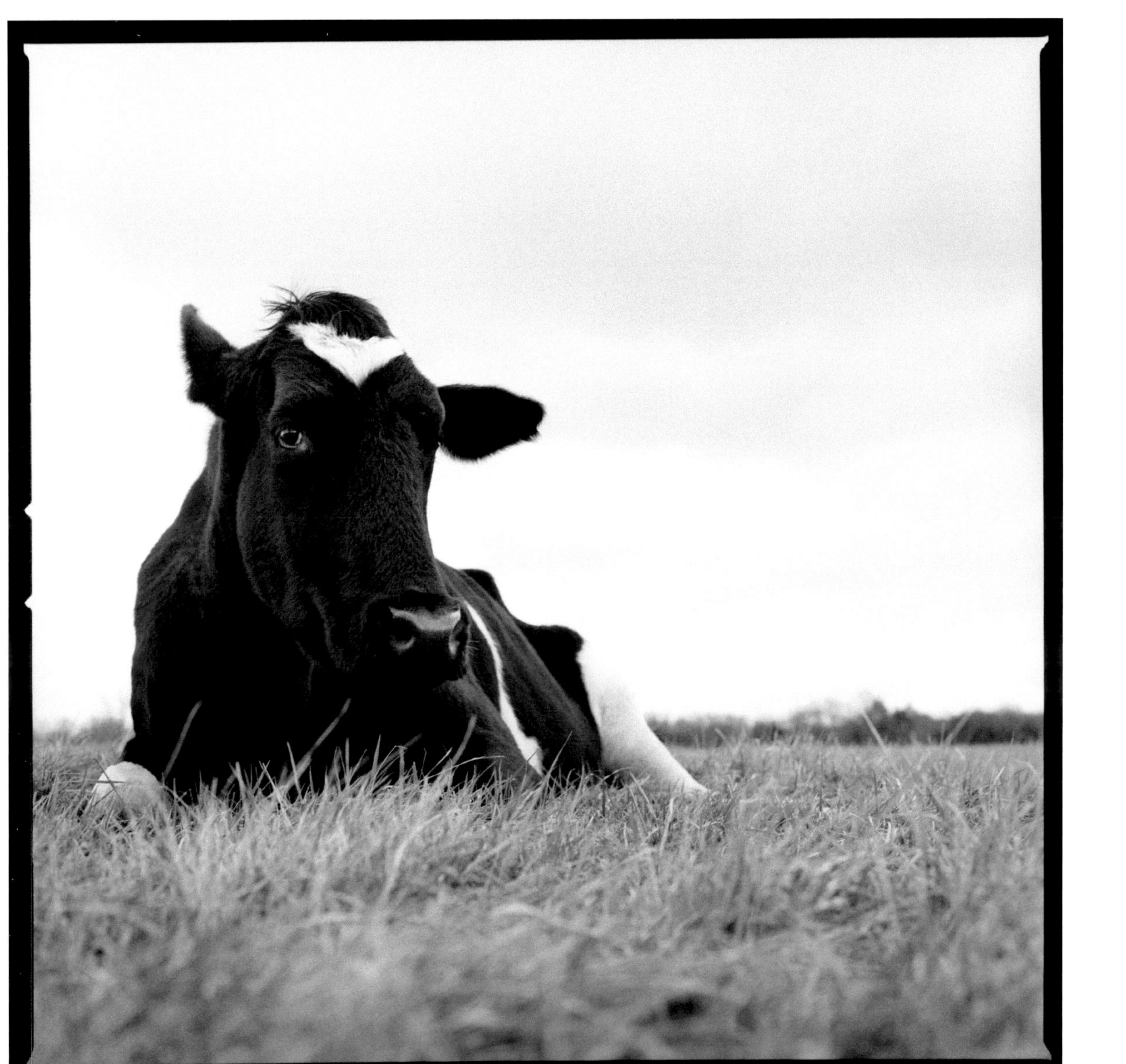

Terrain

Terrain is our oldest Sanctuary Resident. He was the sole survivor of a hatching project and we adopted him as a duckling. Terrain has always lived amiably with our chickens and the other ducks and our peacock Frankincense.

When Donald our Muscovy duck died suddenly of a heart attack one afternoon just after they'd been swimming together, Terrain stood over his friend, nudging him gently and quacking softly. Finally, after getting no response, Terrain sat down beside the dead body of Donald and would not move.

Karen Davis, Founder
United Poultry Concerns

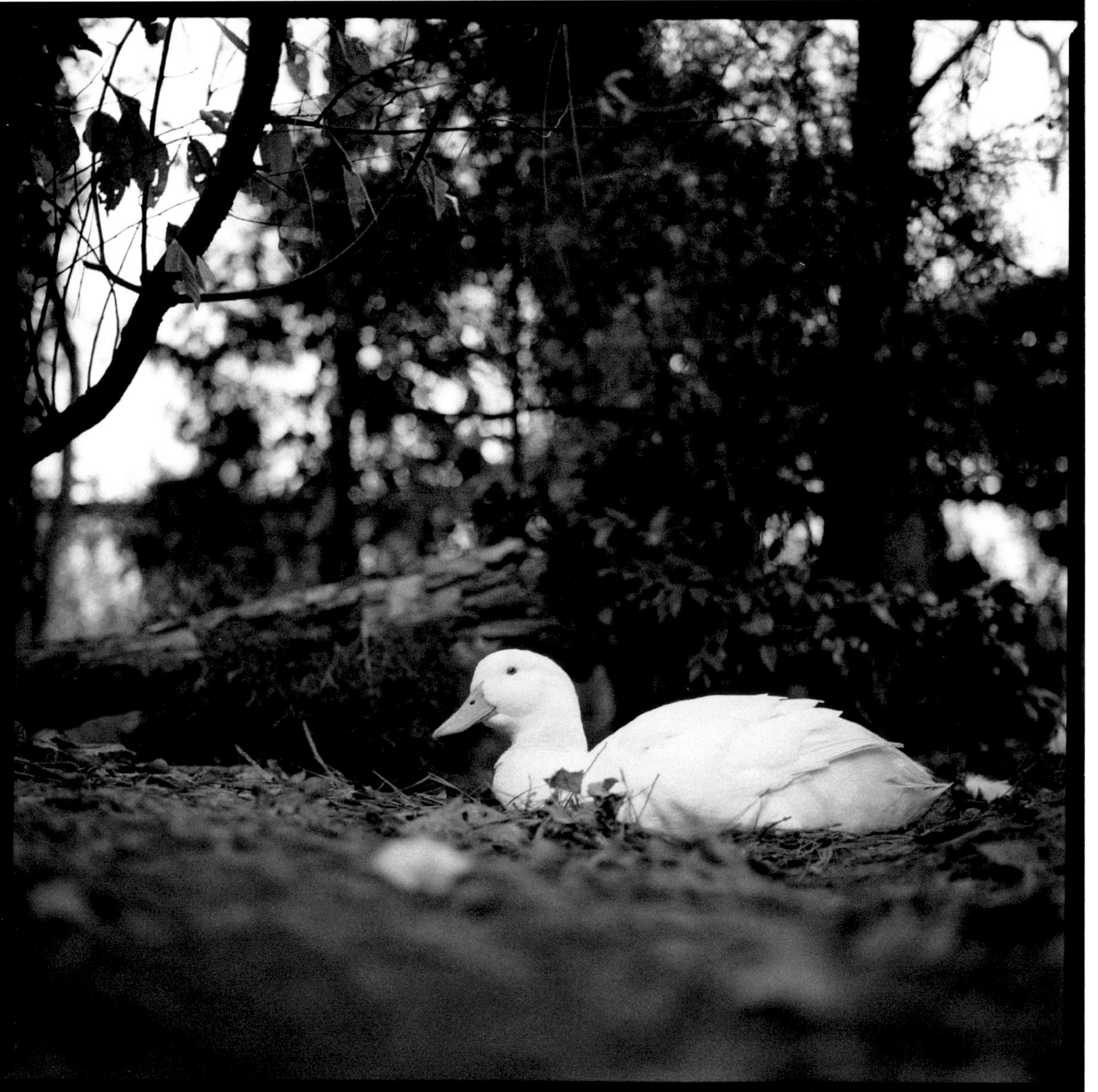

Mr. Newman Goat

In March of 2002 Newman walked up the long driveway of a friends horse farm and announced that he had arrived! No one seemed to know where he had come from, nor where he truly belonged. Apparently that was because this Alpine goat was destined to become the boss at Star Gazing Farm. Newman's antics are known far and wide, and his talents are many: he is an architect, landscape designer, demolition expert, gourmet eater, and a "car guy". He has his own Facebook, Linked In, and Twitter pages, and ensures his hegemony by periodically beating up anyone in his path. He is quite the renaissance goat.

– Farmer Anne, Star Gazing Farm

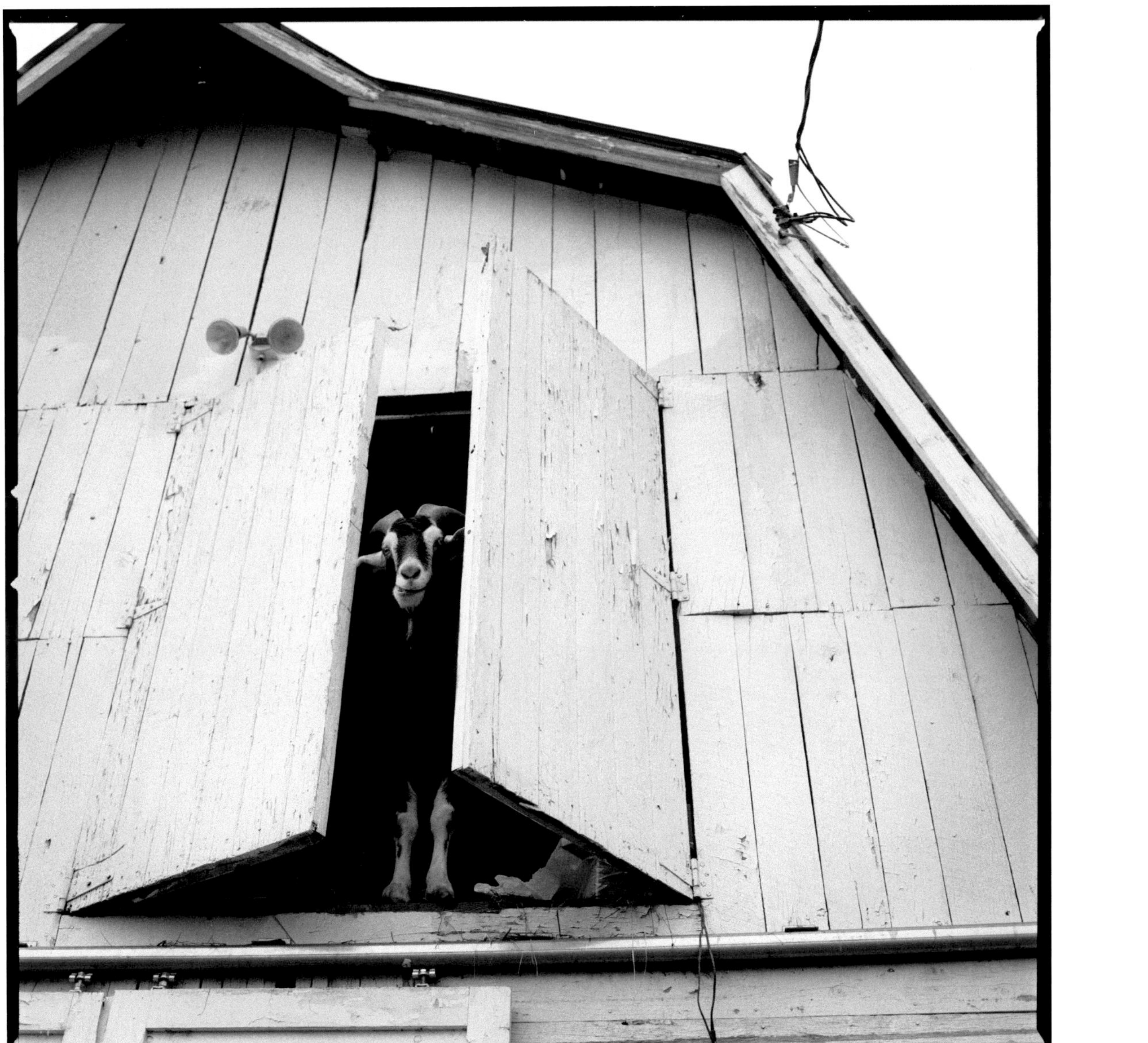

Lacey

Lacey came from a hoarder and had a bad leg, a baby by her side and was pregnant. She had the baby a few weeks after arriving here, a pure white filly we named Lily, the first and only horse ever born here at the farm. We never had a reason to break up the little family, so Lacey has lived here in "the herd" with her daughters ever since. She prefers to be left alone, and we respect that, but her girls are sweet and friendly... so far as any ponies can be considered sweet. (You know, they mostly lean more towards the bratty side.) A couple of times the whole trio were adopted, but they always come back, earning the nickname "yo-yo ponies". At this point we expect them to be here forever!

Shannon Sheridan
Grateful Acres Sanctuary

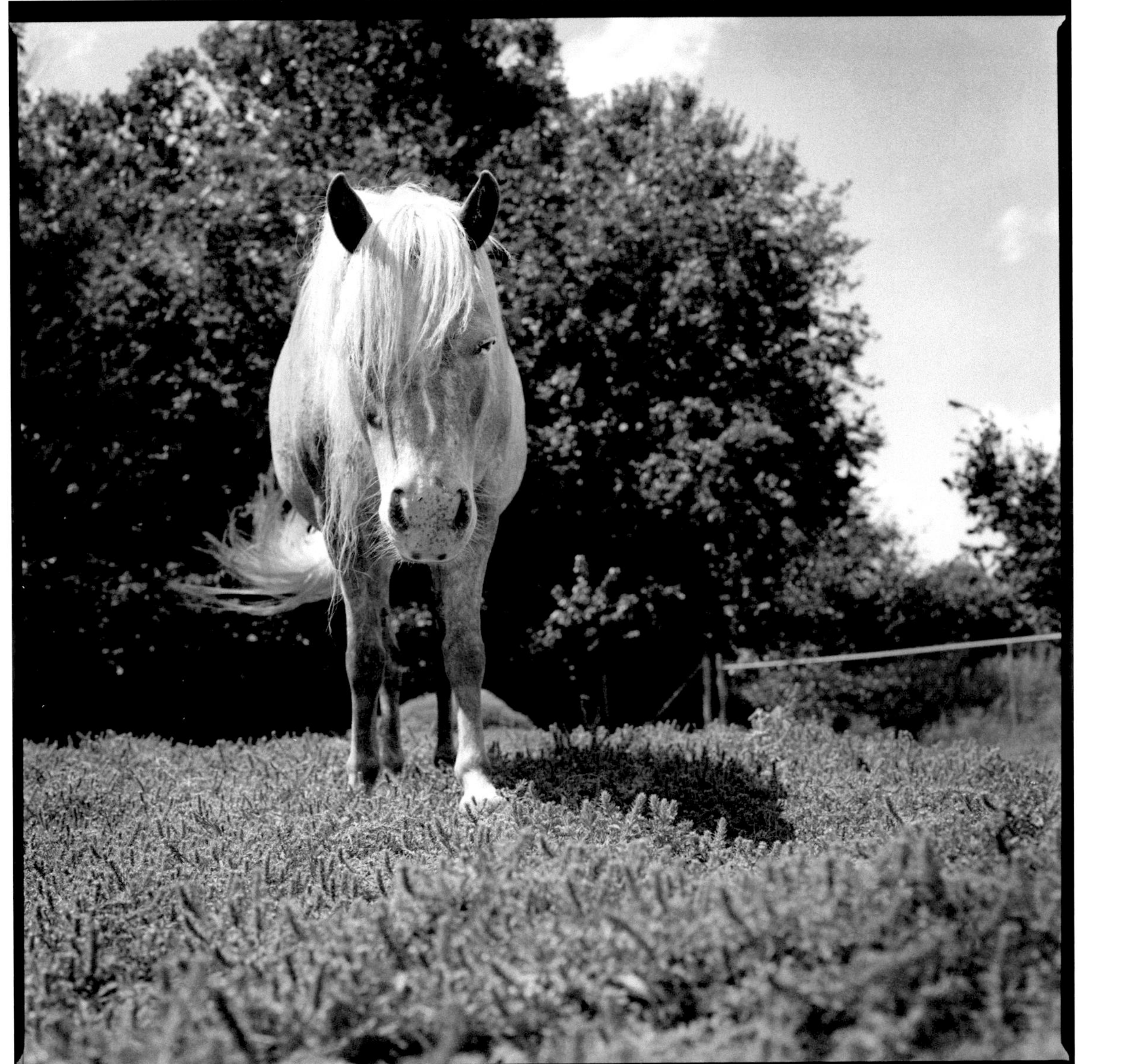

Creating a Sanctuary for Domestic Fowl

Karen Davis

The purpose of our sanctuary on the Virginia Eastern Shore is to provide a home for chickens, turkeys and ducks who need a home, rather than adding to the population and thus diminishing our capacity to adopt more birds. For this reason we do not allow our hens to hatch their eggs in the spring and early summer as they would otherwise do, given their association with the roosters in our yard. All of our birds have been adopted from situations of abandonment or abuse, or else they were no longer wanted or able to be cared for by their previous owners. Our two-acre sanctuary is a fenced open yard that shades into tangled wooded areas filled with trees, bushes, vines, undergrowth, and the soil chickens love to scratch in all year round. It also includes several smaller fenced enclosures with chicken-wire roofs, each with its own predator-proof house, for chickens who are inclined to fly over fences during chick-hatching season, and thus be vulnerable to the raccoons, foxes, owls, possums and other predators inhabiting the woods and fields around us.

Our sanctuary is an essential part of our educational work. Not only is it a refuge for chickens, turkeys and ducks rescued from abusive farming and cockfighting operations, it is an opportunity for visitors to meet our birds while providing the primary sources of information that enable me to educate people through my direct, personal observations. For example, cockfighters like to claim that roosters are "born" to fight, but the roosters at our sanctuary disprove this assertion. The poultry industry wants people to believe that having been "bred" for food, chickens and turkeys can no longer handle the outdoors like their wild ancestors, and therefore they have to be locked up "for their own good". If this were true, how could we explain the fact that here at our sanctuary, these very same birds, who never set foot on the ground before they got here, are vigorously digging in the dirt with their claws, jumping up on tree branches, sunbathing, dustbathing, socializing, showing curiosity, hiding instinctively from foxes and hawks, sounding predator alarms, expressing affection, and doing all the normal things that their wild and feral relatives do? Seen in their pleasant, woodsy surroundings that stimulate their natural activities and reveal their charms, our birds are their own best ambassadors. Many visitors are surprised to see our hens sitting on tree branches. They suddenly realize that chickens are birds! A newspaper reporter who visited our sanctuary a few years ago was surprised to learn that chickens recognize each other as individuals after they've been separated. A friend and I had recently rescued a hen and a rooster in a patch of woods alongside a road in rural Virginia. The first night we managed to get the hen out of the tree, but the rooster got away. The following night after hours of playing hide and seek with him in the rain, we succeeded in getting the rooster, and the two were reunited at our sanctuary. When the reporter visited a few days later, she was impressed that these two chickens, Lois and Lambrusco, were foraging together as a couple, showing that they remembered each other after being apart and enjoyed each other's company.

In reality, chickens form memories that influence their social behavior from the time they are inside the egg, and they update their memories over the course of their lives. I've observed their memories in action at our sanctuary. For instance, if I have to remove a hen from the flock for two or three weeks in order to treat an infection, when I put her outside again, she moves easily back into the flock, which accepts her as if she had never been away. There may be a little showdown, a tiff instigated by another hen, but the challenge is quickly resolved. Best of all, I've watched many a returning hen be greeted by her own flock members, led by the rooster. They will walk over and gather around her conversably, as if to say, "Where have you been?" and "How are you?" and "We're glad you're back."

If there is one trait above all that leaps out to visitors at our sanctuary, it is that chickens and turkeys are cheerful birds. The weather doesn't get them down. Whether it be wind, rain or snow, they're out and about, zestfully pursuing their interests and conducting their daily social dramas in the yard. Their footprints in the snow look like hundreds of wildly trampled peace symbols, and when the white hens who came to us from factory farm cages sit in the branches of a big green bush, they resemble soft candles and magnolia blossoms among the shining leaves.

Karen Davis, PhD is the founder and president of United Poultry Concerns, a nonprofit organization that promotes the compassionate and respectful treatment of domestic fowl. She is the director of a sanctuary for poultry and a writer about these birds. Her articles have appeared in *Animals and Women: Feminist Theoretical Explorations*, the *Encyclopedia of Animals and Humans*, and *Critical Theory and Animal Liberation*. Her books include *Prisoned Chickens, Poisoned Eggs: An Inside Look at the Modern Poultry Industry; More Than a Meal: The Turkey in History, Myth, Ritual, and Reality;* and *The Holocaust and the Henmaid's Tale: A Case for Comparing Atrocities.* She was profiled in *The Washington Post* and is in the U.S. Animal Rights Hall of Fame "for outstanding contributions to animal liberation".

Kaola

Kaola was rescued with several other hens and a rooster named Rupert from a cockfighting ring in Alabama. Upon their arrival at our sanctuary, Kaola immediately joined the other hens in our yard and lived in the Big House with them and three roosters until, some years later, she voluntarily joined a smaller group of just six hens and our easygoing rooster, Mackenzie. She didn't want to be around vigorous young roosters anymore. She preferred the serene atmosphere of Mackenzie's house and has stayed there ever since.

Kaola is a very vocal hen who talks to me when I'm out in the yard. She listens to my voice and looks me straight in the eye with her own beautiful dark eyes whenever I bend down to converse with her.

Karen Davis, Founder
United Poultry Concerns

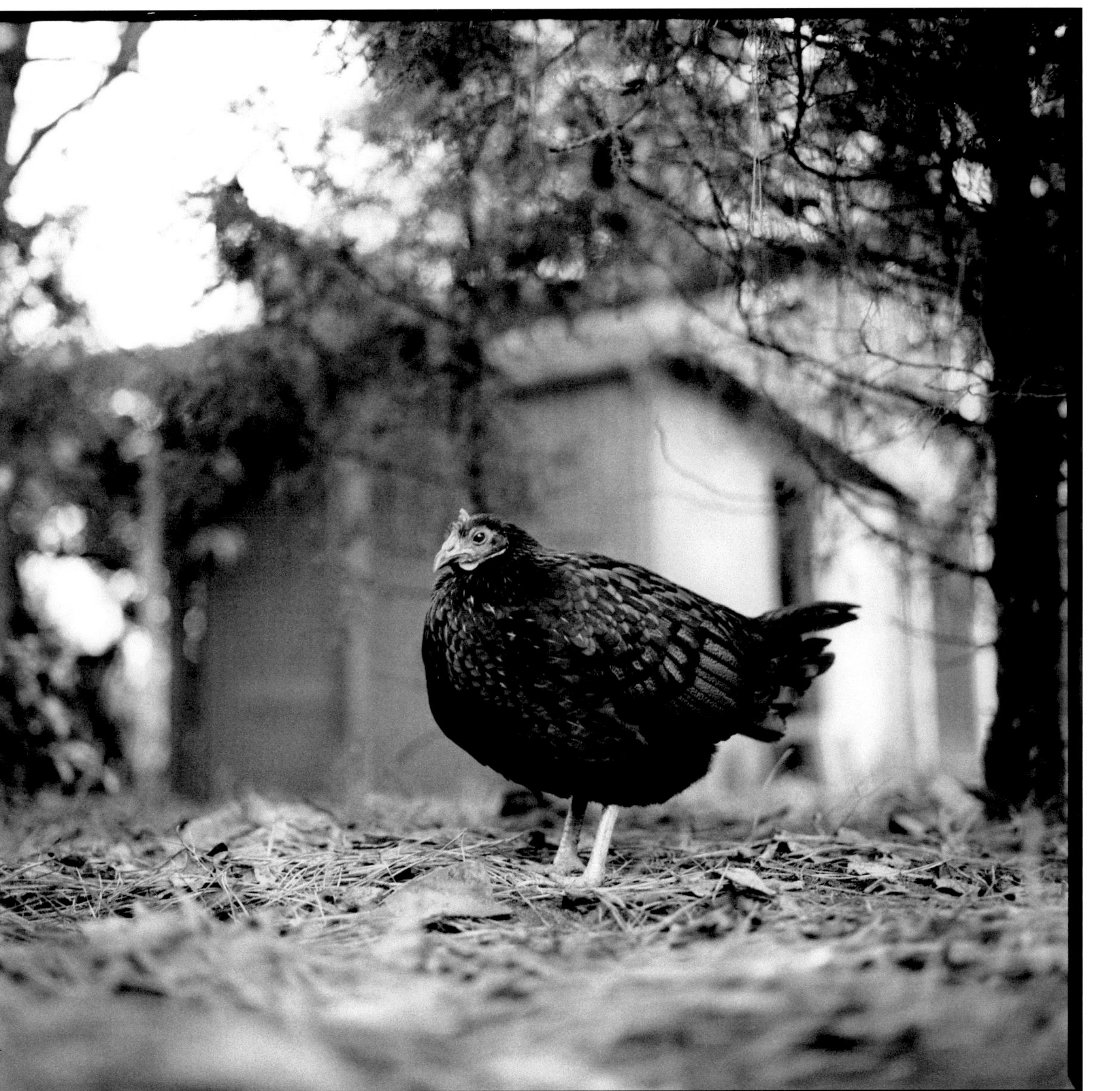

Hickory

Hickory is a Finn sheep, born to a mother ewe who had four babies all at once in February 2006. Two of the lambs died, and Hickory was rejected, his mother deciding she could only handle one youngster. We received a call from the farmer, who told us he wasn't interested in bottle feeding a lamb, so we could "come and get him" if we wanted him. We found him abandoned in the dark in the middle of a farm field, half frozen and crying pitifully.

Upon arrival at the sanctuary Hickory was so cold his body temperature wouldn't register on a thermometer. We put him in a heated water bath, and he slowly warmed up, recovering enough to hungrily nurse on a bottle after a few hours. He was kept in a playpen in the house, and ran around the kitchen wearing diapers, until he had grown enough wool to handle the cold nights in the barn.

Once outside he was like a puppy, following us everywhere, and grew to be strong and healthy. Because he was bottle raised he is one of our friendliest sheep; he will walk up to any visitor wanting to be petted and hugged. He loves running and playing with the other rescued sheep, and his favorite treats are grapes and popcorn.

Terry Cummings Co-Founder Poplar Spring Animal Sanctuary

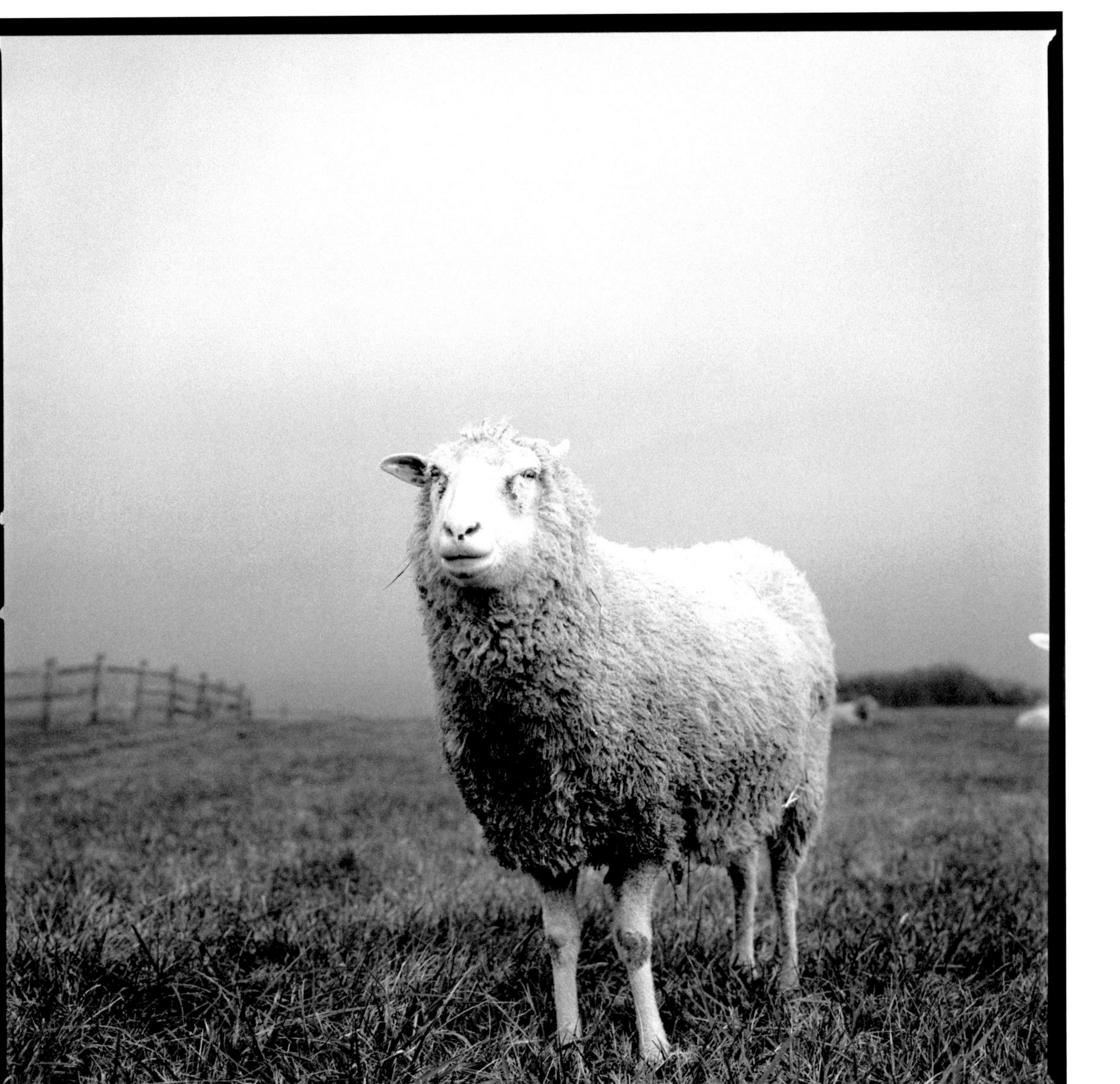

Sebastian

Sebastian will never know the suffering his mother, Juno, once endured. Juno and five other goats were confiscated from a squalid property in upstate New York. Emaciated, crawling with parasites, and limping on their painfully overgrown hooves, these goats were rushed to our New York Shelter for immediate rehabilitative care. When we discovered that all five malnourished females were pregnant, we braced for high-risk deliveries, watching over the expectant mothers 24/7 until they gave birth. To our relief, all delivered successfully. Sebastian and his twin sister Belle were born incredibly small but with a hearty appetite for life. Under the watchful eye of their mother, aunts and human caregivers, these kids have grown into a joyful, rambunctious pair. After playing side by side all day, the two snuggle close together and fall blissfully asleep with their necks crossed.

Gene Baur, Farm Sanctuary

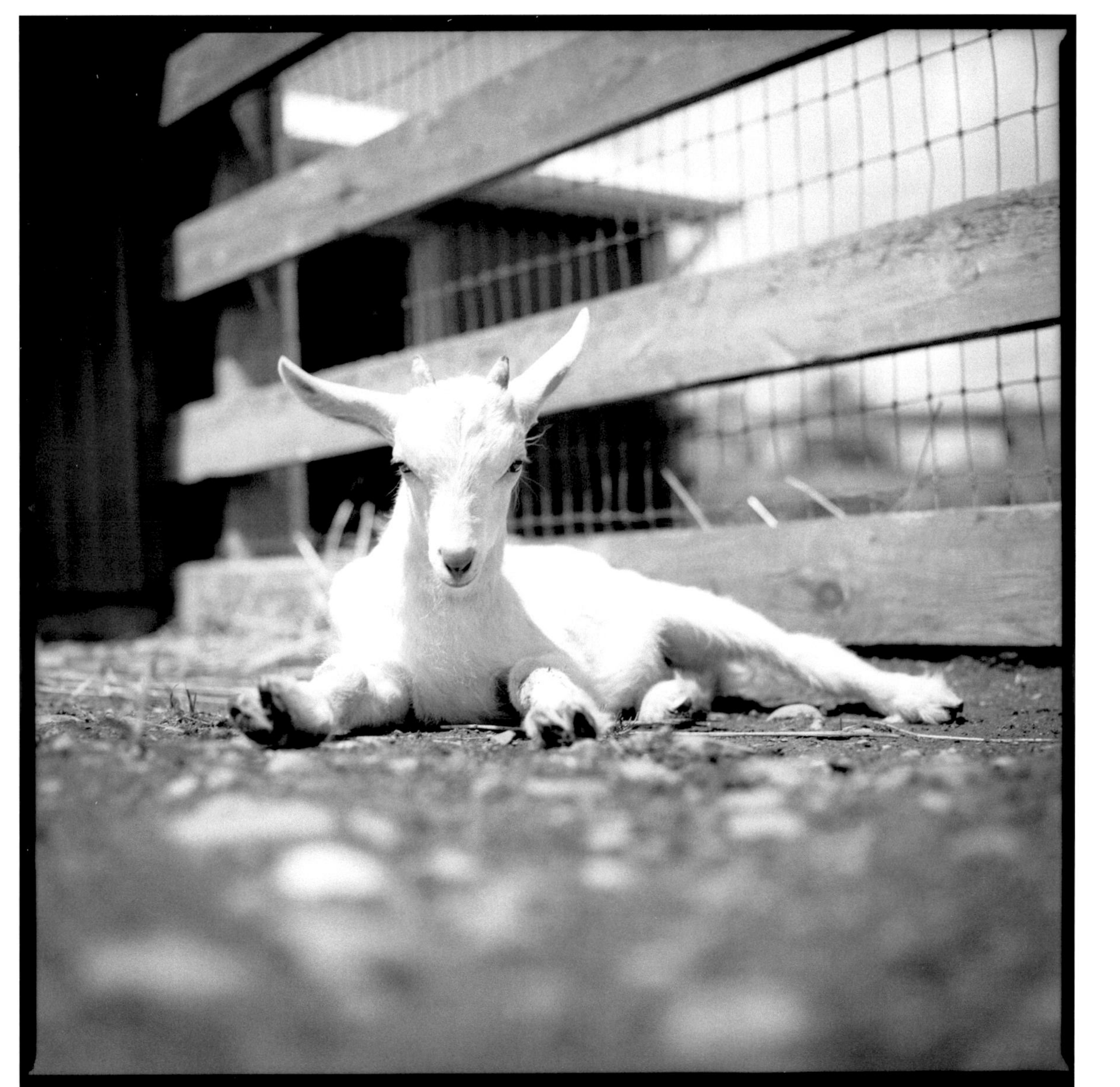

Heidi

Heidi is a beautiful Jersey cow who escaped death three times, once by luck and twice by her own intelligence. She was born on a dairy farm in Georgia, an unwanted byproduct of the dairy industry. In this area there was no market for veal calves, so baby calves were routinely disposed of by being shot and thrown in a pit. Luckily for Heidi the day she was born a goat farmer was giving a lecture to visitors to the farm on making goat cheese, and Heidi was one of four calves given to him as payment.

The farmer brought Heidi and the other calves to his home in Virginia, planning to raise them for beef. When the day came to take them to the slaughterhouse, Heidi ran away into the fields and could not be caught. The farmer tried again a few weeks later, shutting her into a barn and backing the trailer up to the door. But Heidi foiled him once more, jumping out a window and running to safety. When the farmer was overheard by a neighbor cursing and swearing that he would butcher her right on the farm, she decided to purchase Heidi to save her life. She called Poplar Spring and we agreed to take her, but we worried it would be difficult to get her onto a trailer, given her history. Amazingly, even though it was evening, Heidi came out of a big open field and walked right onto our trailer. She has lived happily at the sanctuary ever since. Heidi is sweet and friendly, and very maternal - she has been a wonderful surrogate mother to newly rescued calves over the years, even acting as a "seeing eye cow" to our blind cow, Emily.

Terry Cummings Co-Founder Poplar Spring Animal Sanctuary

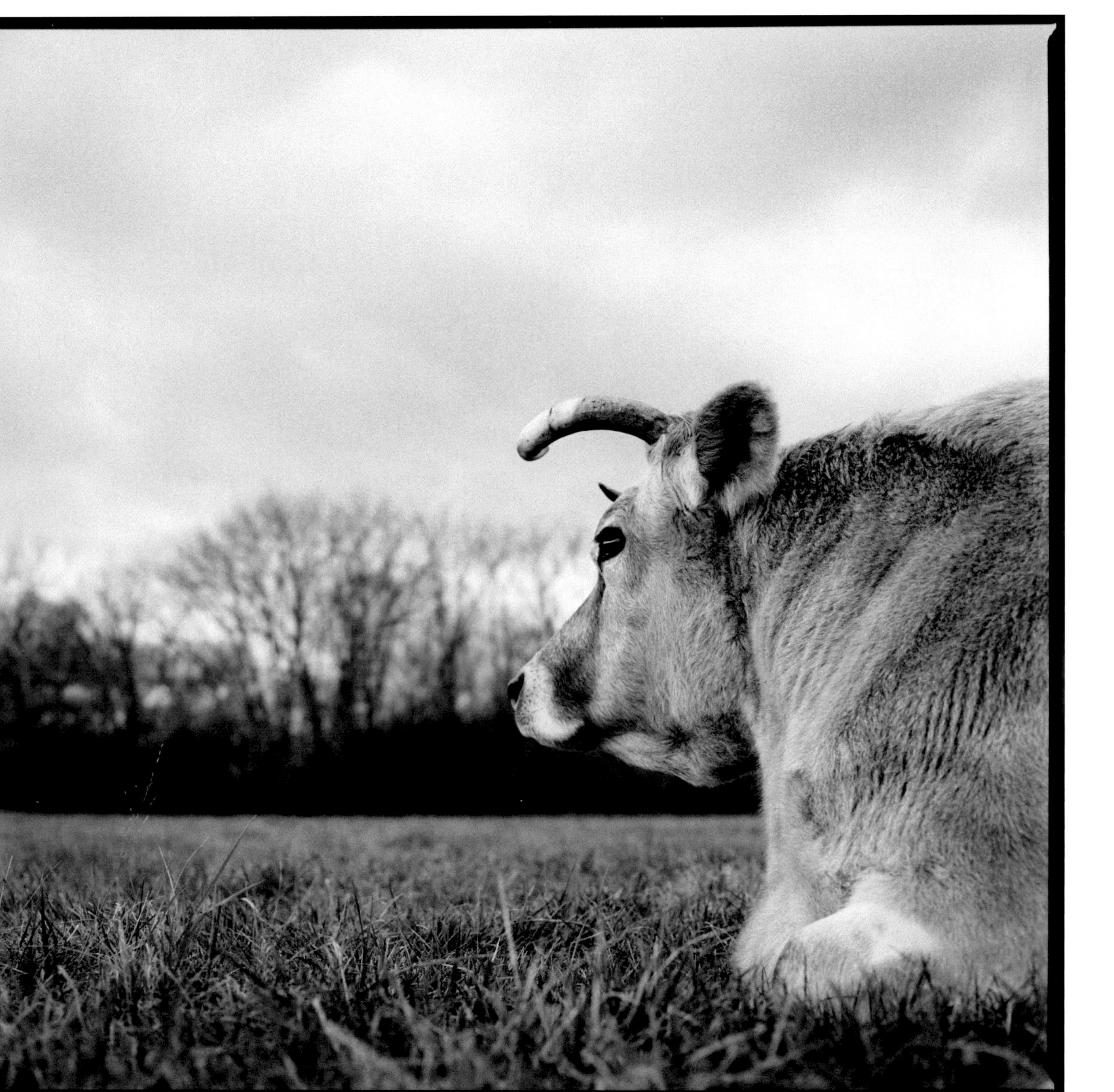

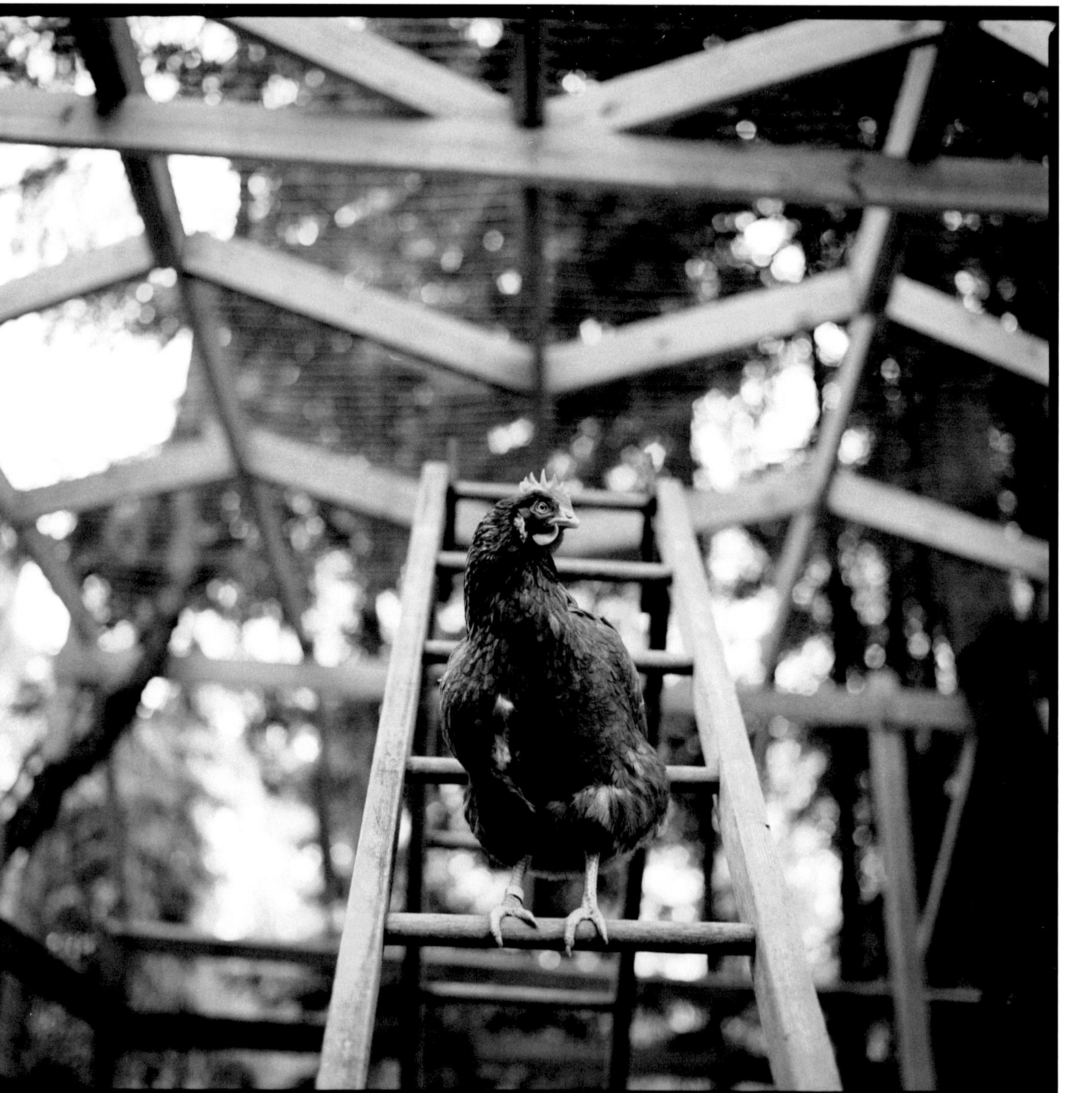

Dee Dee

A homeless man in Harlem felt sorry for the chickens awaiting death in a live meat market. Whenever he could save enough money, he'd purchase a chicken and toss her into a vacant lot. When we heard about the story, there were 18 chickens and two roosters in the lot. They were cold, hungry, and missing many feathers. ASPCA volunteers drove them to us, and within a couple of months they were fully recovered. Dee Dee is one of the chickens. She loves to forage, wandering in the grass and scratching for insects. She flies exceptonally well, and likes to sit on the roost we built for her and her friends. Dee Dee is a happy hen who lays many eggs and makes soothing clucking sounds.

Bill and Ellen Crain
Founders,
Safe Haven Farm Sanctuary

Hannah

Hannah and her son Herbie came to live at the sanctuary after a kind woman saw them and decided she couldn't stand by and watch them go to slaughter.

When Hannah and Herbie arrived at the sanctuary, Herbie was just a baby. But, things have changed for them! Herbie is now in charge of all the sheep and goats, and Hannah is always by his side.

Hannah loves to spend her days hanging out with her son and grazing. Her favorite food is strawberries, with blueberries coming in a close second.

Aimee Pritchard
Kindred Spirits Sanctuary

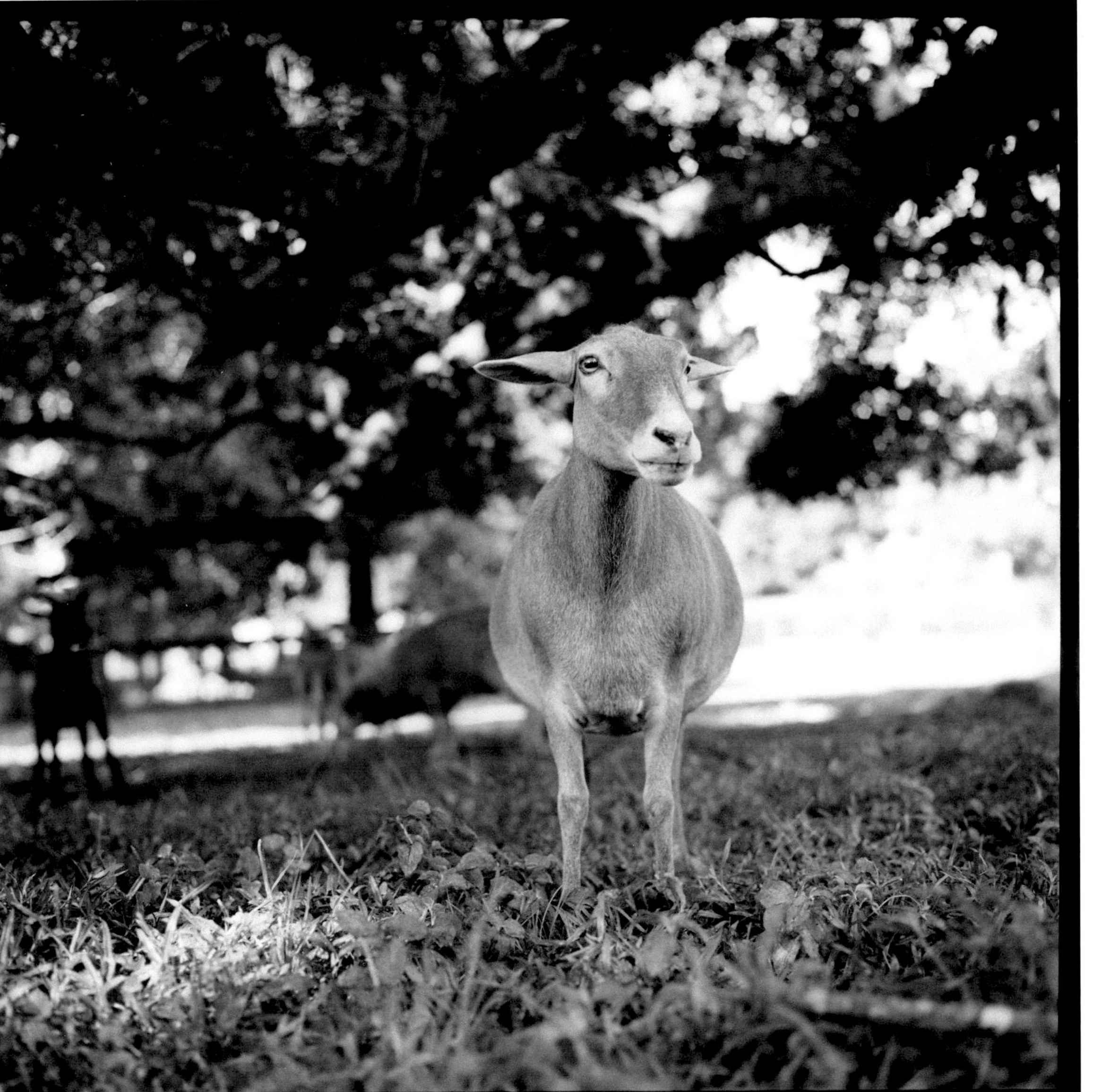

Sadie

One day, four young turkeys were delivered to us. We know little about their life before they arrived. Because much of their beaks and toes had been cut off, the probably began life on a factory farm. These farms cram turkeys and other poultry into such tight cages that they often fight and damage the owners' "products." But instead of giving the turkeys more space, which would eliminate the fighting, the farms sever their beaks and toes - usually without anesthesia.

Another sign that our turkeys came from a factory farm is that the turkeys are entirely white. Consumers don't like any colored pigment on their meat, so factory farmers have created an all-white breed.

Early on, Sadie became the most adventurous of our turkeys. She was first to venture far from the barn, walking 100 yards into a pasture to lay an egg beneath a bush. Sadie also was the only turkey to fly over one of our five-foot fences.

And Sadie showed us how turkeys look out for one another. One day Sadie was lying down in the pasture, preparing to lay an egg, when she heard a noisy fight. One of her friends was fighting with one of the goats. Sadie got up, rushed over to the barn, and helped her friend drive the goat away.

There is, in addition, a quiet side to Sadie. In the evenings when we clean the pastures, she likes to sit still nearby.

Bill and Ellen Crain
Founders
Safe Haven Farm Sanctuary

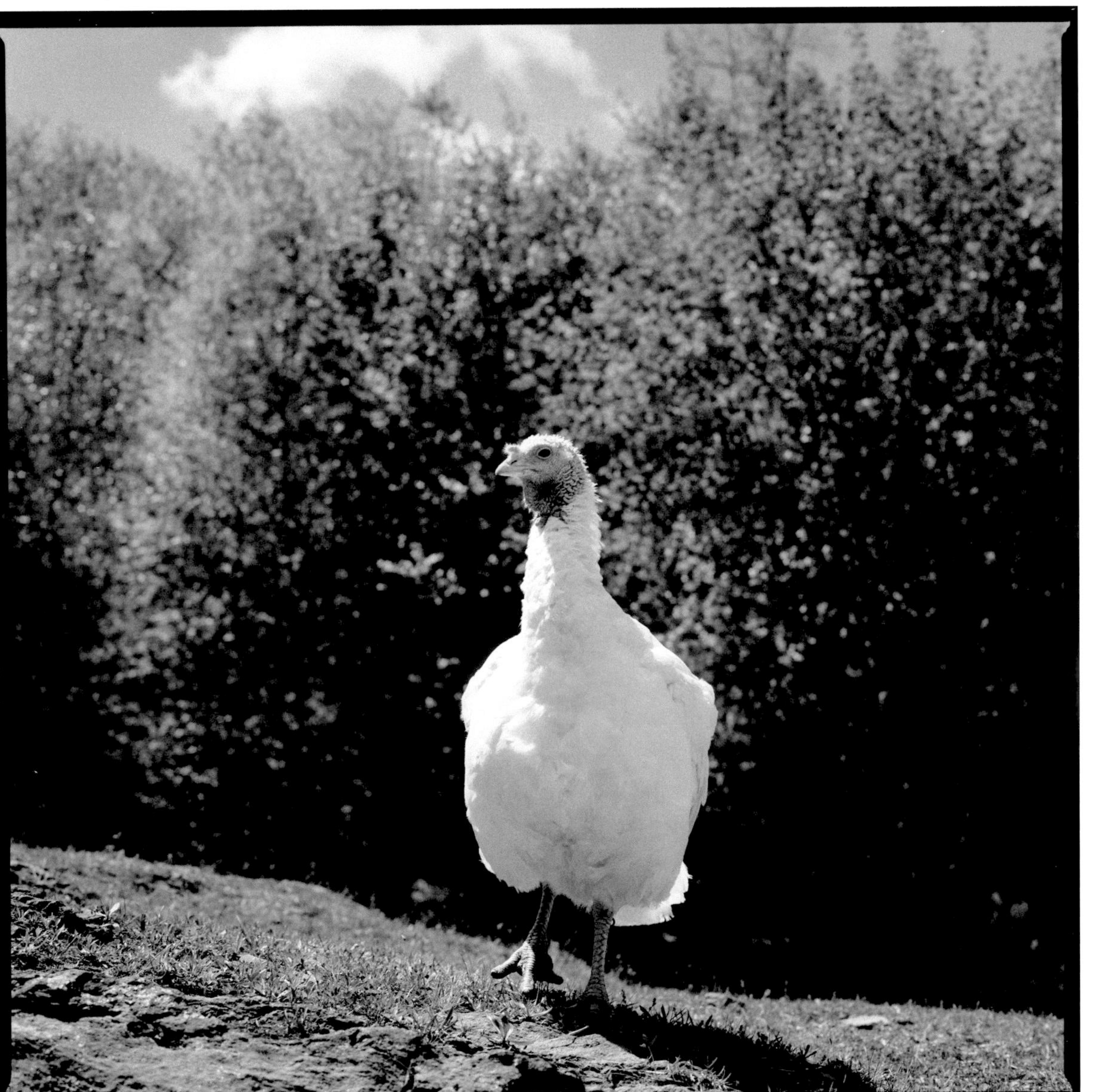

Rocky

Rocky was bottle raised at the Prince William County Animal Shelter Petting Zoo along with Bullwinkle, and was diverted from the road to slaughter by a woman that fell in love with him and arranged for him to come to Star Gazing Farm. Rocky is a purebred Holstein steer (and now at over 4 years old, is considered to be an ox). He stands over 6 feet tall, and is gentle, inscrutable, and serious. Unlike Bullwinkle, he considers his actions carefully and is quite unflappable. He does, however, respond to the high-pitched calls of "Rocky-Boo!" and will do almost anything for a slice of watermelon.

– Farmer Anne, Star Gazing Farm

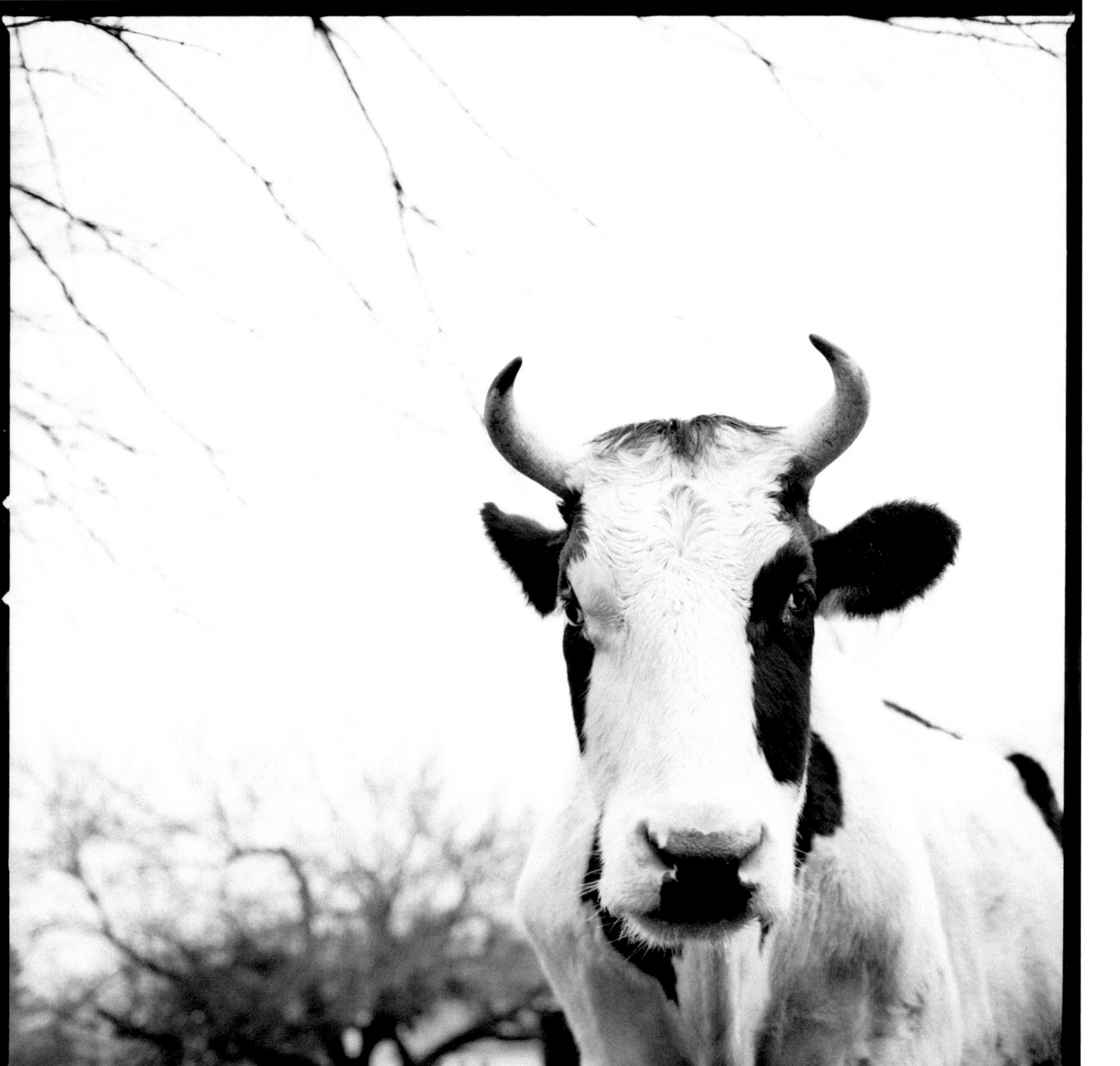

Thomas

Thomas is one of the lucky animals who have only ever known the safety and love of the sanctuary. His mother was very pregnant with him when we rescued her and 14 others from underneath a mobile home.

Thomas and his family spend their days relaxing in the sun, playing in the mud and their nights sleeping side by side.

Logan Vindett
Kindred Spirits Sanctuary

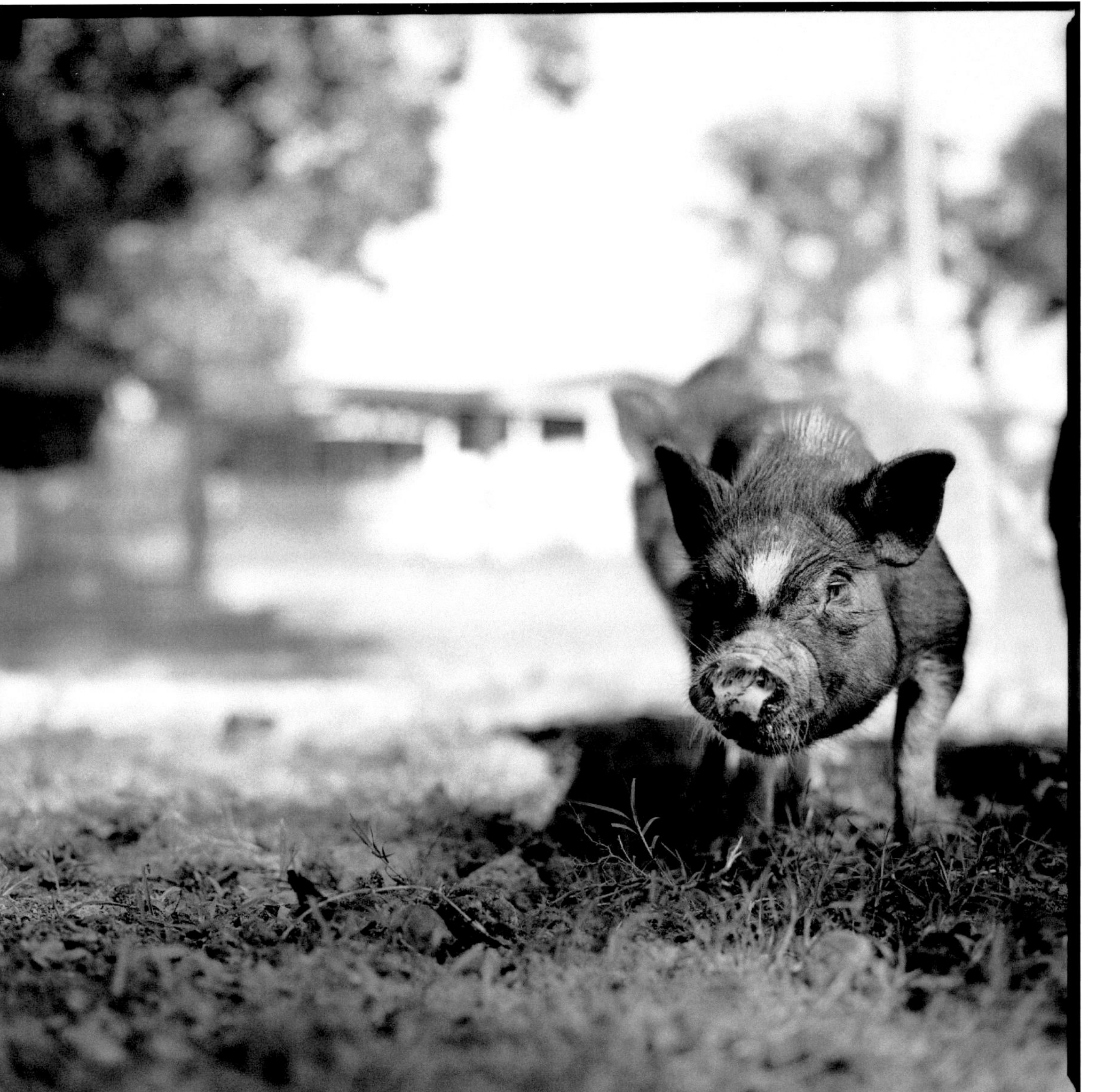

Charles

Charles is a Plymouth Rock rooster who was one of eight chickens raised in a classroom project by a high school teacher. The lesson he was attempting to teach the students is unclear, but when the chicks were a few weeks old he announced to the class that he was planning to slaughter and eat the chickens when they were grown. This disturbed the students greatly, and one of them contacted us, convincing the teacher to release them to Poplar Spring.

Charles grew to be a very proud and handsome rooster, who loves to scratch and peck around the farm with his brothers and sisters. He enjoys dust bathing in the shade under the trees, and his favorite treats are watermelon and canned corn.

Terry Cummings Co-Founder Poplar Spring Animal Sanctuary

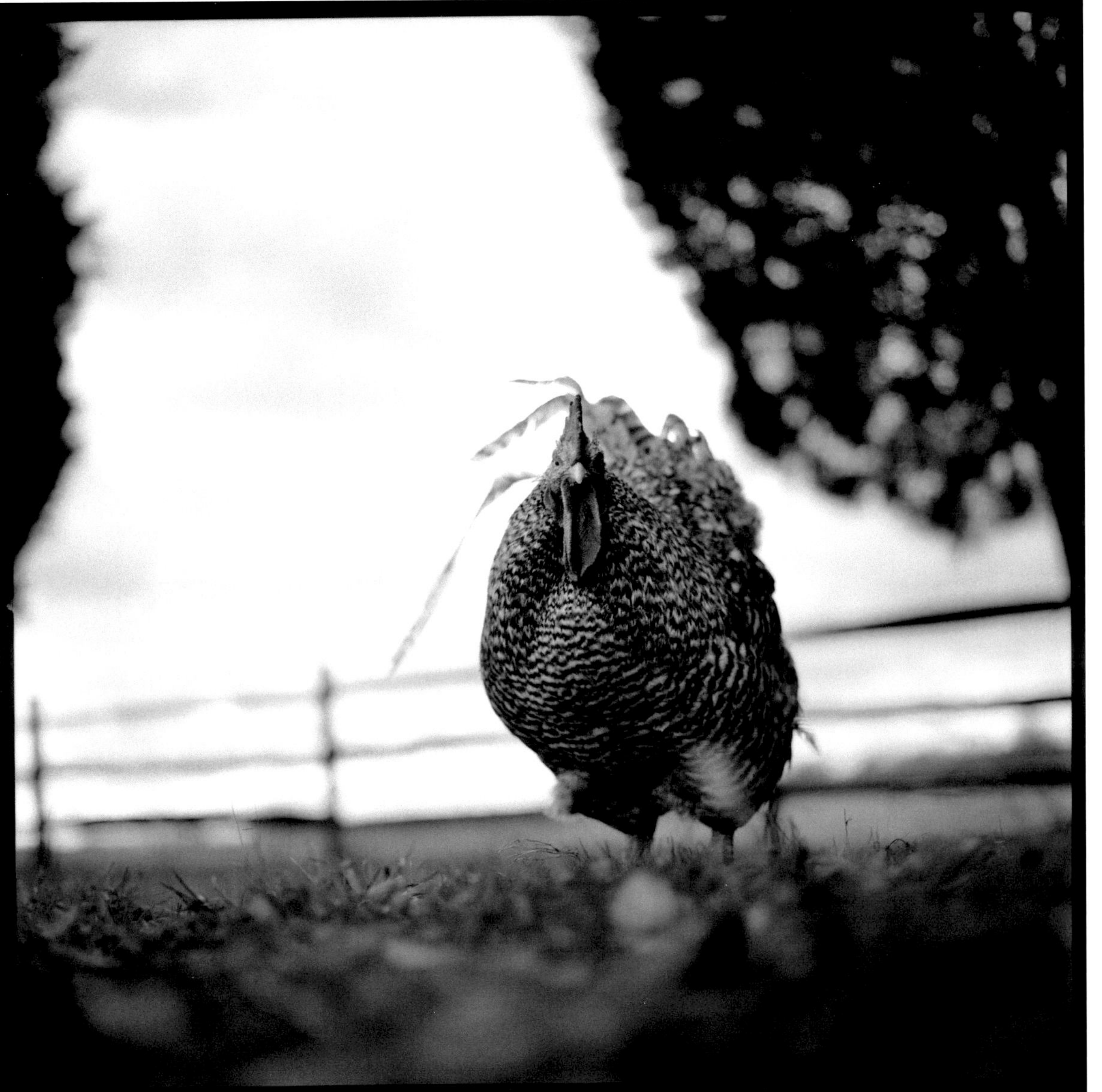

Lilly

Lilly, a stocky gray pygmy goat, came to CAS with her brother Billy when their elderly owners could no longer care for them. Though we were told she'd never been bred, her massive udder swung uncomfortably between her legs like a basketball, nearly touching the ground. One hind leg was shorter than the other, reportedly from a bone infection in her infancy, and she held it crossed behind her in a permanent curtsey.

But we soon discovered that Lilly was no lady. From day one, she was an opinionated firecracker who got a thrill out of hooking unsuspecting humans behind the knee with a well-placed horn. Visitors always got her excited; she'd try to stick her nose in their crotches, snort, waggle her tongue, and make odd blubbering sounds. Considering her eccentric behavior, which is characteristic of a buck in rut, and her huge udder, we concluded that Lilly had some major hormone imbalances. After an unsuccessful round of hormone treatments, she underwent a mastectomy to remove her uncomfortable udder. While her behavior never changed, she was now able to move about more easily - and to wreak more havoc!

Lilly lived out the rest of her life bossing around one of our goat herds, where she could often be found gleefully trying to butt a tree into submission. She gained a large human fan base in spite of - or because of - her loose screws. This charismatic little hellion proved that even the oddest duck is worthy of love.

Abbie Rogers
Former Animal Care Director - Catskill Animal Sanctuary

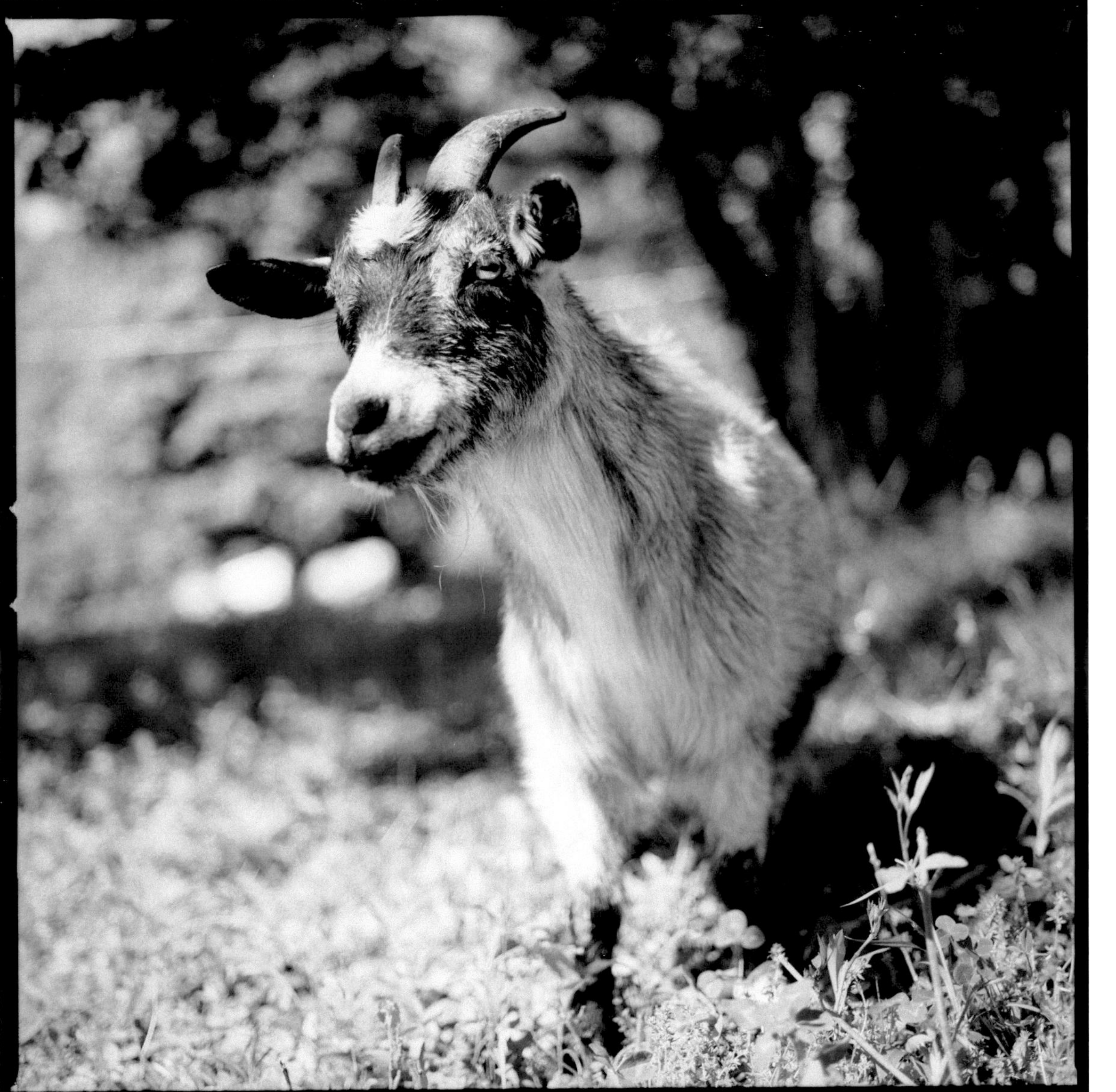

Mickey And Jo

This is Mickey and Jo and they are two wonderful Muscovy ducks. Found by a New York City resident walking her dog in Inwood Hill Park, these two frightened ducks seemed ailing and in distress. Both had the tell-tale sign of having escaped from a local "livestock" operation as their upper bills were cut off. The smaller duck was not using her right wing, and both had extremely pale bills and feet indicating malnourishment. A friend of Woodstock Farm Animal Sanctuary and some of our dedicated volunteers managed to catch the ducks. The smaller duck was immediately taken to a vet. In examining her injuries, the vet surmised that she was hurt by being brutally kicked or hit in some way. Sadly, her wing had to be amputated. Soon after, the two ducks were brought to Woodstock Farm Animal Sanctuary. Upon being reunited, their joy and relief was palpable. They ran toward one another making excited but gentle noises and lay their necks around each other as if embracing. To this day, they remain inseparable. Now named Mickey and Jo, both are doing wonderfully! Jo gets around just fine with her one wing. Due to the nurturing care, food, shelter, vitamins and love that they are now given at the sanctuary, Mickey and Jo enjoy a peaceful life swimming in the pond and hanging out with their friends.

~Jenny Brown and Doug Abel
Co-Founders, Woodstock Farm Animal Sanctuary

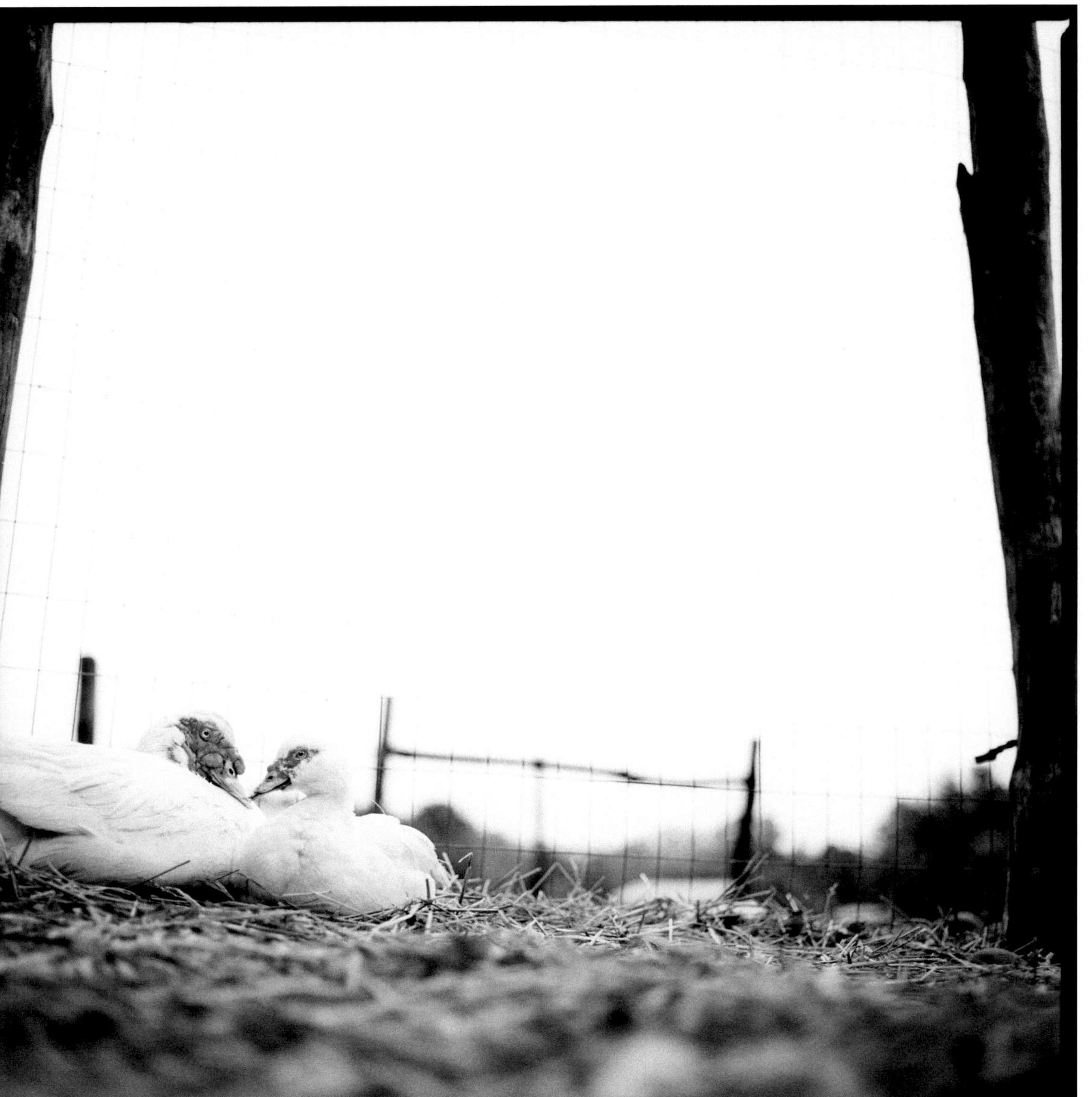

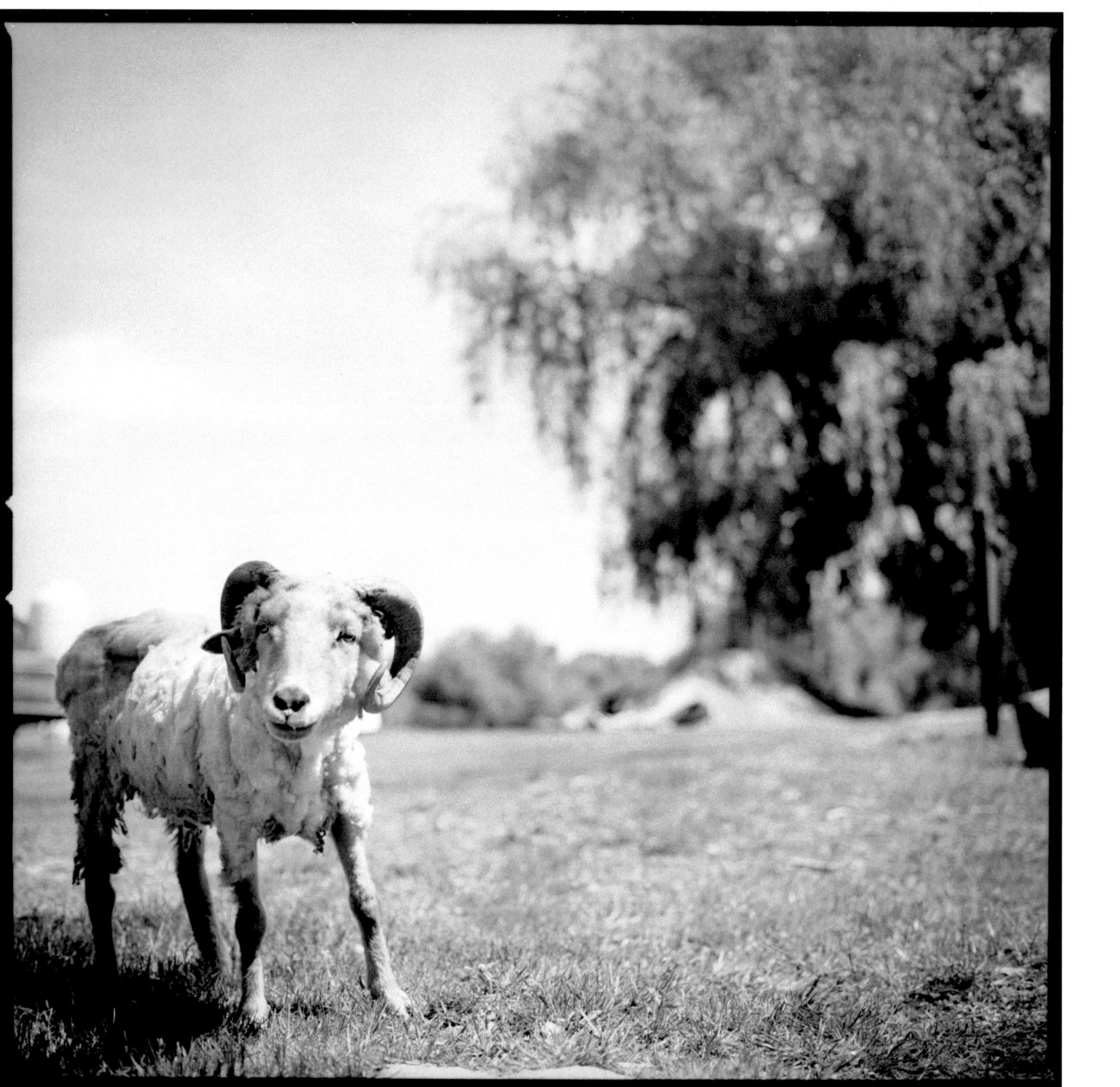

Tribute to Aries

Kathy Stevens

In the ten years since our founding, Catskill Animal Sanctuary has taken in nearly 2,000 needy farm animals. The greatest joy of our work is participating in the transformation of broken spirits, as we try through every word, gesture, and action to say to our new charges: "You are safe here. You can count on us." The greatest difficulty, of course, is saying goodbye to those whom we have cared for and loved, and yet there is such beauty, and many lessons, in these moments as well.

Aries arrived at Catskill Animal Sanctuary in 2004 with 40 other animals from a failed sanctuary. He was a small, beautiful sheep, with loose, curly wool, enormous, penetrating eyes, and a gentle, unassuming nature. For years, Aries lived with his best pal Lumpy and the rest of his flock in a large pasture at the northern end of our property. In ones and twos, the flock shrank: a pair was adopted; two elderly sheep died. And over those years, both Lumpy and Aries became old men who eventually earned a coveted spot among the Underfoot Family, the ever-changing group of animals who live in our main barn and who, during the work day, do essentially whatever they choose...which is generally to be underfoot. Among all the creatures who reside at CAS, it is the Underfoots whom we know most intimately. We weave through them — these sheep, goats, chickens, turkeys, even the occasional horse — as we clean stalls, rake the barn aisle, lead other animals out for the day. We shoo them from the kitchen after they've maneuvered their way inside in the hopes of raiding feed bins; we kneel to offer kisses or strokes of the head to animals peacefully resting in a pile of hay.

For two years, Aries was a beloved member of this family. In a gang of enormous personalities, the kind and self-possessed Aries was a refreshing counterpoint: tranquil, composed, a perpetual smile on his face.

———

It had been two bitterly cold days since Aries left his stall; two days since he ate any food offered him. This morning, though, was warm and sunny, and our farm manager marveled as she watched Aries struggle up on shaky legs, hobble down the long aisle, and slowly circle the barn.

"Kathy, I'm not one of *those* animal people," Sara said to me later. "But I think he was saying goodbye."

Along his way, he must have spoken with his friends, for when he returned to his stall, they followed him in: Barbie the hen, Atlas the goat, and Lumpy. Barbie lay no more than three inches in front of Aries' face. We humans have no idea how they knew, but it appeared to us that the entire Underfoot Family seemed to know that their friend was leaving.

When I walked in the barn, Dr. Rosenberg was standing outside Aries' stall. Aries looked quite comfy in a pile of fluffy hay; staff and volunteers were with him. When I walked to the door, Aries stood and moved purposefully toward me until we simply couldn't be any closer, and I was overcome by the love that radiated from the gentle beast. That he was aware of and at peace with what was imminent was not unusual — others before him have been as well. What was unusual were his efforts, all morning long, to say goodbye to the beings who were his friends.

"I love you, friend," I whispered. As Aries grew sleepy from the initial injection, some of us offered quiet memories, words of love. Others simply held him. When he was ready, Mark gently shaved a small patch of wool from his neck and injected the solution that would stop Aries' heart. More soft words and tender hands enveloped the old sheep.

For a few hours, we left Aries' body in the stall so that his animal friends could do what they needed to. When we returned from lunch, Atlas, the special needs goat, was lying between Aries' front and rear legs, his head resting on Aries' belly. The birds rested in a semi-circle around the two friends.

On his final day, this unassuming sheep with a perpetual smile showed us what he was made of. Peace. Wisdom. Dignity. Gratitude. Astounding grace. When my time comes, I hope I possess the strength of character to leave as he did: acknowledging and thanking those I loved for sharing my journey, and letting them know that on the next leg, I will be just fine.

Kathy Stevens, founder and director of Catskill Animal Sanctuary, spent her childhood on a Virginia horse farm, years that instilled in her a deep love of and respect for all animals. She moved to Boston in the late 1980s, received her master's degree from Tufts University, then spent eleven years as a high school English teacher. In 2000 she was invited to become the principal of a new charter high school. Instead, one year later, she opened Catskill Animal Sanctuary. In ten years, CAS has become one of the nation's leading sanctuaries for farmed animals, and with the launch of its children's camp and vegan cooking program, a powerful voice for compassionate living. Kathy's books, *Where the Blind Horse Sings* and *Animal Camp*, share the life-changing lessons learned from a blind horse, a sheep, a rooster, and a pig, and received much critical and popular acclaim. Kathy lives behind the barn with her dog Hannah and her cats Fat Boy and Mouse.

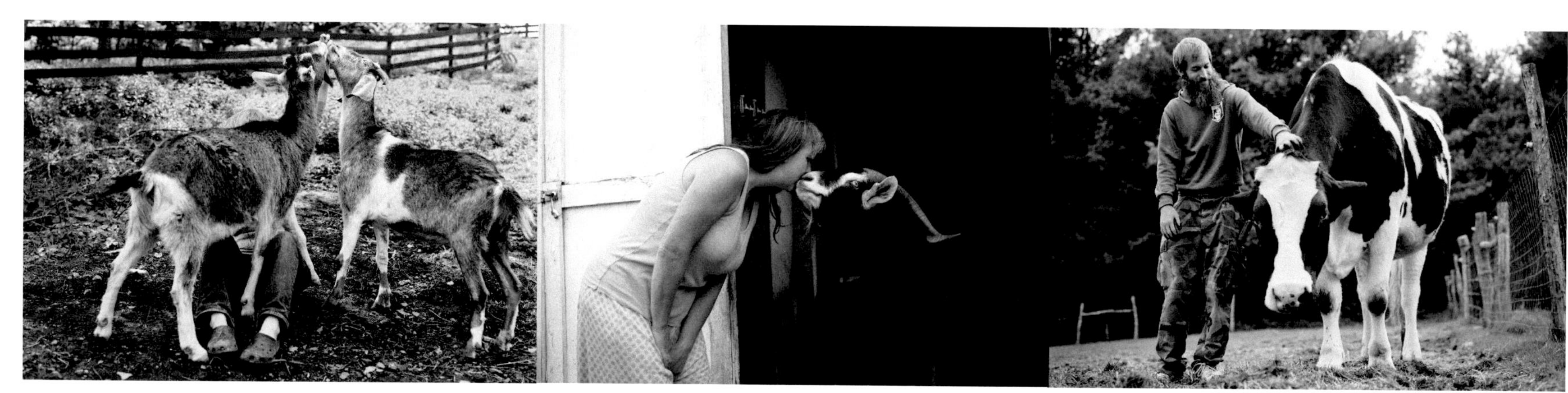

Resources

Sanctuary Info
Farm Animal Shelters: www.farmanimalshelters.org
Catskill Animal Sanctuary: casanctuary.org
Farm Sanctuary: www.farmsanctuary.org
Kindred Spirits Sanctuary: www.kindredspiritssanctuary.org
Poplar Spring Animal Sanctuary: www.animalsanctuary.org
United Poultry Concerns: www.upc-online.org
Safe Haven Farm Sanctuary: safehavenfarmsanctuary.org
SASHA Farm: www.sashafarm.org
Star Gazing Farm: www.stargazingfarm.org
Woodstock Farm Animal Sanctuary: woodstocksanctuary.org

Organizations
People for the Ethical Treatment of Animals: www.peta.org
In Defense of Animals: www.idausa.org
Compassion Over Killing: www.cok.net
The Fund For Animals: www.fundforanimals.org
Mercy For Animals www.mercyforanimals.org
Humane Society of the United States: www.humanesociety.org

Books
Where the Blind Horse Sings: Love and Healing at an Animal Sanctuary by Kathy Stevens
Farm Sanctuary: Changing Hearts and Minds About Animals and Food by Gene Baur
The Pig Who Sang to the Moon: The Emotional World of Farm Animals by Jeffrey Masson
Eating Animals by Jonathan Safran Foer
The Dreaded Comparison: Human and Animal Slavery by Marjorie Spiegel
Thanking the Monkey: Rethinking the Way We Treat Animals by Karen Dawn
Dead Meat by Sue Coe and Alexander Cockburn
Prisoned Chickens, Poisoned Eggs: An Inside Look at the Modern Poultry Industry by Karen Davis

For additional resources and photographs relating to this project visit: farmanimalsanctuaryproject.com

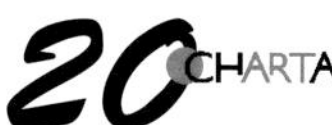

To find out more about Charta,
and to learn about our most recent
publications, visit

www.chartaartbooks.it

Printed in April 2012
by Bianca & Volta, Truccazzano (MI)
for Edizioni Charta